PEOPLE

YOUR GREATEST ASSET OR BIGGEST HEADACHE?

Additional books by Leon Drennan:

Seasons of the Soul – Which one are you in?
Good King / Bad King – Which One Are You?

PEOPLE

YOUR GREATEST ASSET OR BIGGEST HEADACHE?

LEON DRENNAN

Vision Leadership Foundation
Brentwood, TN

Published by Vision Leadership Foundation, Brentwood, TN 37027
© Copyright 2015 Vision Leadership Foundation. All Rights Reserved.

Any form of duplication—physical, digital, photographic or otherwise is expressly forbidden, unless authorized in writing by the author/publisher.

ISBN 978-0-9904033-2-6

Scripture quoted in this book comes from one of the four sources noted below. Unless otherwise noted, the default verson for use is the New American Standard Bible.

Scripture taken from THE HOLY BIBLE, ENGLISH STANDARD VERSION® (ESV®) Copyright © 2001 by Crossway, a publishing ministry of Good News Publishers. Used by permission. All rights reserved.

Scripture taken from the KING JAMES VERSION, public domain.

Scripture taken from the NEW AMERICAN STANDARD BIBLE®, Copyright © 1960, 1962, 1963, 1968, 1971, 1972, 1973, 1975, 1977, 1995 by The Lockman Foundation. Used by permission.

Scripture taken from THE HOLY BIBLE, NEW INTERNATIONAL VERSION®, NIV® Copyright © 1973, 1978, 1984, 2011 by Biblica, Inc.® Used by permission. All rights reserved worldwide.

The contents of this book are based on my recollection and understanding of Scripture as inspired by the Spirit and by a lifetime of leadership experience in a large, complex organization, as well as on the observation of others in leadership roles. My thoughts have been influenced by some great books and Christian authors as referenced in this book. Any perceived similarities to leadership or management materials in the marketplace are coincidental except those which I have specifically cited. — Leon Drennan, Vision Leadership Foundation

For more information about Vision Leadership Foundation, please visit:

www.Vision-Leadership.com
or, contact Leon Drennan at leon@vision-leadership.com

Dedication

This book is dedicated in loving memory of my mom and dad, who taught me to work hard, persevere, and pursue God. Also, to my children Scott, Allyson, and Kelsey—in birth order. They bring me great joy and gave me three good reasons to persevere. Finally, and most importantly, to my wife Debbie who has loved me unconditionally for thirty-eight years and who has persevered with me. She is my greatest single joy on this earth.

This is also dedicated to a very dear friend, Gerald Stow. Gerald loves, encourages, and builds up people better than anyone I know. I have learned much from him. He's encouraged me many times. I consider it a privilege to call him my friend. He is one of God's unexpected and undeserved special blessings in my life.

Acknowledgments

I appreciate the Frist family and all the leaders at HCA, too many to mention by name, who allowed me to serve and learn in a great organization for thirty-one years. I thank Diana Rush, my executive assistant of many years and trusted friend, who worked a full-time job and helped in her spare time with formatting and graphics in this book. Thanks to Jim Baker, Brian Ball, Debbie Drennan, Louis Joseph, Mark Rainey, Joe Steakley, and Vail Willis, who read this and gave me such valuable feedback. Finally, I thank all my past colleagues, employees, peers, and associates for the fun we had together, what I learned from them, what we accomplished together and, most importantly, for their friendship. Also, a big thank you to Scott Drennan and Darrel Girardier for their inspiring work and design of the book cover. A special thanks goes to Fred MacKrell at AuthorTrack.com, who guided me in every major phase of this project. Thanks also for adding his creativity to the graphics and layout of the book.

PEOPLE

Table of Contents

Preface vii
Introduction ix

Part I	**Giving People What They Need** 1	
Chapter 1	Meaning 5	
Chapter 2	Empowerment and Freedom 9	
Chapter 3	Security 15	
Chapter 4	Honor 19	
Chapter 5	Friends 25	
Chapter 6	Compensation 27	
Chapter 7	Direction, Connection and Context 29	
Chapter 8	Clear Priorities 37	
Chapter 9	Balanced Priorities 43	
Part II	**Getting What You Need** 47	
Chapter 10	Know Your People 49	
Chapter 11	Understand People's Personalities (Their Hardwiring) 57	
Chapter 12	Choose the Right Team 77	
Chapter 13	Make Sure People Still Fit Their Jobs 91	
Chapter 14	Avoid Common People Mistakes 99	
Chapter 15	Help Under-Performers 105	
Chapter 16	Influence Motivation 111	
Chapter 17	Influence People Through High Expectations 121	
Chapter 18	Delegate Effectively 129	
Chapter 19	Create a Culture That Empowers 137	
Chapter 20	Lead Change 143	
Chapter 21	Document and Train 153	
Chapter 22	Create Enabling Control Systems 157	
Chapter 23	Create Progress Through Measurement 163	
Chapter 24	Summary 169	
	Credits and Endnotes 171	

PEOPLE

Preface

I've always been fascinated with people, leadership, and organizations. I learned about these through growing up on the family farm, hauling hay as a teenager, working in a factory, and (during my college years) working in a rock quarry serving for over thirty-five years in business, church, and nonprofit organizations, and studying the leadership of kings in the Old Testament and the life of Jesus, the King of Kings.

I realized as a young man that my calling and passion was to develop leaders and help improve organizations. I worked for thirty-one years at Hospital Corporation of America (HCA), the largest for-profit hospital company in the world. I was blessed with the opportunity to lead in a variety of executive roles which allowed me to lead auditors, construction and engineering professionals, nurses, doctors, and others. I had the opportunity to serve in my last twelve years as President of HCA Physician Services.

My calling and passion never changed though I wore many different hats and worked with people in many different professions in my career. I loved developing people and building, redefining, and improving organizations.

Although my division was maturing and growing fast, I started sensing God leading me to make a move. I swallowed hard and, in faith, started making plans to leave the company where I had spent most of my adult life. It was one of the hardest things I've ever done. My transition took a couple of years before I left HCA and was ready for the next phase of life.

I formed Vision Leadership Foundation in 2010 with a goal to mentor, coach and train leaders using what God has taught me through many years and varied experiences. This phase involves developing leaders and helping organizations function better in the business, non-profit, and ministry sectors. The goal is to help leaders:

- Get more done in less time and with less frustration and stress.
- Create more profitability (if they are business owners) so they have more financial resources to contribute to ministries and charities.
- Have more time for their spouses, children, churches, communities, friends, and enjoyment of life.
- Create healthy organizational cultures to benefit their employees rather than bringing difficulty and stress into their lives.

I have a growing desire to be able to give more to ministries and charities. I believe that through helping others I can do more for ministries and charities than I would have ever been able to do myself.

If you can't handle people, you can't lead an organization. This book is about what people need, how to give it to them, and how to get what the organization needs in the process.

Introduction

> **Thought:**
> Are you using people or engaging them?

THE LEADER'S ROLE

One role of a leader is to steward the assets of the organization to achieve its mission. The parable of the talents makes clear a leader's responsibility to steward resources available to them. Another role is what King David realized in 2 Samuel 5:12 (KJV):

> *"And David perceived that the Lord had established him as King over Israel and that he exalted his kingdom for His people Israel's sake..."*

So, which comes first, being a good steward of the organization's resources or being a blessing to the people? I will contend that you can only be a great steward of the organization's resources if you are a blessing to people, especially the employees.

Let's think this through. If you had an organization that was highly automated, could you be prosperous and a good steward if you did not optimize the use of the machines and treat them with great care in terms of maintenance, repair, etc.? Yet, some leaders who would take great care with expensive equipment tend to ignore or even abuse people, the greatest asset in any organization.

Leading Isn't Easy

No one I've ever known that had any real experience in the field has said that leading people is easy. Moses got so frustrated with the children of Israel that at one point he essentially said, "God if you going to treat me this way, just kill me." God got so angry that He wiped out everyone on the face of the earth with a flood and spared only Noah and his family.

There's no doubt that people can be and are very frustrating at times. The bottom line is, what are you going to do? Will you look at people as God ultimately does? Yes, there were times when He wanted to eliminate people. But, you can only understand God's true and lasting heart toward people when you see the cross in the background and how He gave his Son so we could have a relationship with Him. If you see people primarily as a headache rather than an asset, then your organization is not going to be very prosperous and, frankly, you're not a very good leader. The New Testament says that to seek to be an overseer is a worthy ambition. Leading people is challenging to say the least. The question is whether you have the heart and the head for it.

The Right Heart

What kind of heart do you need? I remember a story of a relatively young man. He was washing his bright red sports car at the public car wash. He attracted the attention of a nine-year-old boy. The young lad peppered him with questions such as, "Mister, you must work a lot of hours to own a car like that!" to which the young man replied, "No, I don't work a lot of hours."

The boy said, "Then, you must have a really high paying job to own a car like that." The young man replied, "No, son, I don't have a high-paying job."

The boy scratched his head, thought, and said, "Well then, you must own the company to be able to own a car like that" to which the young man replied, "No, son, I don't own the company."

To avoid further questioning he said, "Look, son, I don't work a lot of hours, I don't make a lot of money, I don't have a big job, and, in fact, I don't even have a job. The truth is my big brother bought me this car."

The little boy looked down and kind of pawed at the ground with his foot. He stuttered and said, "Mister, I wish, I wish, I wish." The young man, sure he knew what the young boy would say, was going to go ahead and finish the thought for him. Something along the lines of "I know. You wish you had a big brother like that." Before he got it out, the boy finished his sentence and said, "Gee, mister, I would sure like to be a big brother like that." The young man was stunned and carried that response with him the rest of his life.

I hope you carry this thought with you as well. If you don't truly have in your heart the desire to be like a big brother, to do something extraordinary for somebody else, please get out of the business of trying to be a leader!

The Right Head

Though Moses had a good heart and was working himself to death to hear the disputes of the people, he wasn't blessing the very people he was trying to lead. They were standing in long lines wasting their days in the hot desert waiting on Moses. Later, Moses took his father-in-law's advice and ceased trying to do it all by himself. Then he actually blessed them by organizing, delegating, and training.

Leading only with the head can be cold and harsh. Many kings of the Old Testament proved that. But leading with the heart without the head can be very dysfunctional. Moses certainly proved that. Good leadership takes both.

Think of people you know who are all head. What kind of culture exists in their organization? Think of someone you know who is all heart. What is the culture of their organization? Think of someone who has a good balance of both head and heart. What is their organization like? Think about where you are on the scale. Are you where you want to be? If not, what would you have to change to be there?

I'm thinking of three leaders. One was a founder. One got fired. One failed. The founder was in the middle. He founded and led a highly successful corporation for many years. He had an excellent balance of heart for people and head for organizational life and business. He disciplined himself to think of ideas regularly to improve the lives of employees, but at the same time he is one of the smartest, shrewdest business people that I know.

The persons who got fired led primarily with the head but with little heart. They were nice people. But, they were not well-balanced. Under pressure, they went purely for the results and watched out more for themselves than for other people. They got fired. I've observed many that fit this category and ended with the same fate over time.

The person who failed was a leader who led mostly with heart. He really cared about people but did not understand organizations, did not understand priorities, and did not stay focused on the mission. Because he could not stay focused, follow through on commitments, and be held accountable, his organization imploded.

Part I

GIVING PEOPLE WHAT THEY NEED

"Give and it will be given to you. A good measure, pressed down, shaken together and running over, will be poured into your lap."
Luke 6:38 (NIV)

Which comes first? Do I get what I need from employees for the organization and then try to meet their needs? Or do I meet their needs and then get what I need for the organization? Our answer to that will shape our attitude toward employees, our actions toward them, their reactions toward us, the whole human relations dynamic, and the overall productivity and culture of the organization.

The position of this book is that you have to give people what they believe they need in order for them to give the organization what it needs. Scripture says, "Give and it will be given to you." (Luke 6:38).

The question now becomes, what do people need? I say the following based on my experience.

Meaning

People need to be part of something bigger than themselves and beyond themselves. They need to know that they matter and why. Until a leader shows a person why they really matter to the organization, what the organization wants doesn't matter much to the person other than for a paycheck.

Empowerment and freedom

People need to be empowered so they have a sense of freedom to act within broad guidelines with appropriate accountability.

Security

It's hard to do a good job and look over your back at the same time. People need to be secure in their work.

Honor

People need to be valued by their superiors, peers, and others.

Friends

People need enough social interaction to be excited about the team they're working with.

Fair compensation

People need to be focused on doing the job to the best of their ability and believe they are fairly compensated.

Connection and context

People need to be connected to something larger than themselves that they are passionate about. They need to understand the context they are operating in to see if they can support the organization and contribute meaningfully to it.

Clear priorities

People need to know they're working on something that is important and that their focus will not constantly be shifted.

Balanced priorities

People need to be able to achieve goals that give them a sense of awareness and balance in all areas of life.

It's my contention throughout this book that leaders who meet these core needs of people get the most and best out of employees. The great thing about it is they get the best because that's what the employee wants to give. It's not manipulated or forced out of them.

PEOPLE

Chapter 1

MEANING

> **Thought:**
> When people ask you how they can make a real difference in the organization, or "Where are we going?" can you answer them?

"You have been called for this purpose . . ."
1 Peter 2:21

People desperately need to know they matter and why! "God has a purpose for each life He creates, and each purpose is as unique as the individual's fingerprint."[1] God created everything on purpose and for a purpose. "I want to make a difference." That's the most frequent statement I've heard in thirty-five years of my professional career. In interviews, people say, "I want to make a difference, I want to have an impact, and I want my life to count." There are many other ways they say it, but it all means the same thing. They want to matter—to have meaning and purpose. They say it in organizational meetings, in annual reviews, and in everyday life in the hallways. I've heard it literally hundreds of times.

> *Everyone has his own vocation or mission in life; everyone must carry out a concrete assignment that demands fulfillment. Therein he cannot be replaced, nor can his life be repeated, thus everyone's task is as unique as is his specific opportunity to implement it.*[2]
>
> —Viktor Frankl

Making a Difference

I saw Mark a few weeks ago. He was really tired. After he told me about his schedule, I understood why. He was putting in a lot of hours and hard work. I was curious as to why he didn't do something else. He is very qualified and could make a good living with other companies without the long hours and intense schedules. I asked him why he was doing this. Actually, he was setting the pace and putting the expectations on himself. The reason he was working so hard was because he saw a window of opportunity to really make a difference in the lives of people through his project. He believed it would improve the quality of healthcare for patients and make a difference for the company. When the discussion was over, it all boiled down to one thing: He genuinely wanted to make a difference.

I'm also reminded of Janine. She's not a high-level executive in a healthcare company like Mark. She is a lower-level employee with a company that helps dry out buildings after floods or any kind of water damage. She came to my house on the Saturday following the great flood of Nashville in May 2010 when she was supposed to have the day off, after already working 14 days in row. I had some flooding in the basement, and she remembered something that she wanted to check. She came to my house, not for the money, not to further a career, and not for the recognition. She came because she cared about people and their lives and wanted to make a difference. And sure enough, she found an area of mold which had been overlooked. She did make a difference!

Your purpose

God made us to serve a purpose in His world. Why wouldn't we have a strong need for meaning and purpose? Viktor Frankl, in Man's Search for Meaning, made the point that people in concentration camps who found a purpose for living—a reason why their lives counted—survived, while those without purpose died much more quickly.[3] When they created a purpose for survival, which was always associated with helping others who were weaker and sicker, they lived much longer. There is a reason why Rick Warren's The Purpose Driven Life sold over thirty million copies.[4] People are genuinely interested in their purpose.

What's that got to do with life in corporate America, churches, ministries, and non-profit organizations? I've seen enough in all those types of organizations to be convinced people are slowly dying emotionally and physically from their lack of impact. The lack of impact I'm talking about is people working really hard without clear direction and meaning. They don't have a clear understanding of what God designed them to do in this world, how they have a meaningful impact on the organization, or how they work for the betterment of other people.

People don't work just for money

I remember a study done about meaningful work. The going rate for ditch diggers was $10 per hour at the time. In this study ditch diggers were hired and paid $12 per hour. Needless to say, this attracted a lot of attention. The first day, the diggers were paid $12 per hour for digging a ditch. The next day, they filled in the ditch and were paid again. This was the routine: dig a ditch one day and fill it in the next for $12 per hour. After a few days, the workers began to lose interest. They lost half the workforce. They raised the pay to $15 an hour, 50% above the market for ditch diggers. After a few days of the same routine, half that workforce left. This continued until the pay for digging and filling in a ditch was $25 per hour, two and half times the going rate. Finally, no one was willing to work even at this rate. Why? When the workers were interviewed, it was discovered the extra money wasn't worth it because they lost all sense of meaning in their work. Digging a ditch only to fill it in again served no useful purpose. And the workers weren't willing to do it.

> *A man can bear any what if he has a big enough why.*
> —Friedrich Nietzsche

The *why* Nietzsche refers to is really meaning or purpose in life. Purpose matters! I have seen firsthand in business and ministry that people will give their lives to achieve a meaningful purpose. Some are willing to die for a great cause—purpose. People are willing to work only so hard in a job, but they will give their all for a great purpose.

> *We are never really happy unless, and until, we are moving toward the accomplishment of something that is important to us.*
>
> — Brian Tracy

People who don't see *meaning* in what they are doing will ultimately not be as productive as those who do. Instead of being an asset, they may be a *headache* for leadership

What are you doing to show your people they matter?

Chapter 2

EMPOWERMENT AND FREEDOM

> Thought:
> Are you limiting the growth of your organization because you fail to empower people?

"Then the Lord God took the man and put him in the Garden of Eden to cultivate it and keep it."

Genesis 2:15

> *"Then teach them the statutes and the laws, and make known to them the way in which they are to walk and the work they are to do.*
>
> *Furthermore, you should select out of all the people able men who fear God, men of truth, those who hate dishonest gain; and you shall place these over them as leaders of thousands, of hundreds, fifties and tens. Let them judge the people at all times; and let it be that every major dispute they bring to you, but every minor dispute they themselves will judge. So it will be easier for you, and they will bear the burden with you.*
>
> *If you do this thing and God so commands you, then you will be able to endure, and all these people also will go to their place in peace. So Moses listened to his father-in-law and did all that he had said."*
>
> *Exodus 18:20-23*

I have noticed a tendency for small businesses to hit barriers and stay small. Non-profit organizations spring up everywhere but only a few get large. There are mega-churches in the United States, but most churches are small, under one hundred people. Why is that? Why do so many businesses, churches, and other organizations tend to plateau and seem unable to grow any further? The key is how they approach the use of power. Are they going to approach it like Moses did when he started out? He kept all the power, and people gathered around him waiting for him to judge their cases and give them direction. Or, are they going to approach it the way Jethro suggested to Moses? That way was to identify capable leaders, provide training, and empower them to act on most cases, keeping only the hardest cases for himself—management by exception.

Today, we might refer to these approaches as the "mom and pop" or sole proprietor versus the franchise. As I grew up in a small town, I observed the sole proprietor approach at the local grocery and hardware stores. They had few employees, and everything revolved around the owner. HCA gave me the opportunity to experience a different style of leadership, one common in large companies and franchises. In the first instance, the power is retained by the owner or the founder. In the second, power is distributed to a number of other people. It works the same way in large, sophisticated organizations as it does in a franchise organization.

THE LIMITATIONS OF KEEPING THE POWER

Small businesses and organizations stay small because the focus is on the owners/founders. They always have ownership and control of the organization. We see this model throughout society. We deal with local businesses, and the owners are always there making the decisions. When they're out, the employees have to call or wait for them to return before making a decision outside the norm.

When organizations are led only in these ways, they never outgrow what the individual leaders can touch. What's the difference between a person owning and running one restaurant and the same person owning and running ten, twenty, thirty, or even one hundred restaurants? With some basic skills in the restaurant business, people can run a single restaurant. However, to run ten restaurants or one hundred, they have to approach it much differently, like a franchise. What makes franchises[5] and large organizations like HCA different? A lot of things such as the following:

- Operating manuals for each key aspect of the organization indicating how things are to be done.
- Measurement of certain key activities and standards for what is expected.
- Checks and balances so that activities have an acceptable level of control but are not stifled.
- Information technology and management reporting so that the leaders can know what's going on without always being there physically to observe.

Franchises require goals for individual business units and goals, coupled with good training, for each position in the organization. They have great policy and procedure guides, operating manuals, training systems, and control systems. Managers are carefully selected and trained to operate successfully within acceptable boundaries.

In this model, like the one I experienced at HCA, goals are established. People are empowered to operate within these goals. There are policies and procedures in place to empower decision-making but also to guide it. This model is not dependent on the leader's continual presence day-to-day. People know what to do and how to do it, and they are empowered within certain guidelines to take action.

Let's compare this to a river. Rivers have movement. They have power. It is very easy to get caught in the current of the river and be swept way. Rivers have direction. Rivers have banks, which are boundaries that give the river direction. Likewise, goals give individuals power and movement. Vision and priorities give direction. Policies and training give them boundaries, just like the banks of a river.

BLESSING PEOPLE BY EMPOWERING THEM

How are people blessed in organizations that empower them? First of all, they have clear goals and are empowered to act without always being told what to do or with someone always looking over their shoulder.

I remember one of my direct reports, who lived out of state, saying that he had received four e-mails from me in two years and all of those were responses to his e-mails. He said, "I don't think I could ever accuse you of micromanaging." This was a very capable leader who had a clear set of goals. All he needed from me was occasional support and discussion to answer a question. God instilled a need for freedom in people. He runs the universe by giving people clear directions. He gave an operating manual, the Bible, to guide and instruct us. And the Holy Spirit is available for day-to-day specific guidance. God gives His people a great deal of freedom but with guidance and accountability.

People like freedom, need freedom, and seek freedom. God gave man great freedom when He created him. Man could eat from any tree in the garden except one. When you hire people who can achieve their personal goals by doing what they're called to do while using their gifts and passions to do what they want to do and what your organization needs done, you can give them great freedom. It's like water flowing in the river. They just naturally fit and flow with the organization. I've observed that when employees become dependent on their leaders to take action, it causes a great deal of frustration and anxiety. They don't feel the same sense of ownership and control of their lives as when they're given clear goals consistent with what they want to do and are empowered to act, knowing they have their leaders' support.

Also, it's hard for people to be efficient if they spend too much time each day waiting for leaders to give directions or make decisions for them. They feel drained. On the contrary, people feel energized when they've had a productive day.

When dependency on the leaders is reduced, the team feels more empowered, more free, is more productive, and has higher morale because people feel like they have a level of control and trust. They feel more like kids than adults when someone is always looking over their shoulder. People don't always like being told what to do by their leaders, particularly people with personality profiles like mine.

Let's look at a simple example. Companies have expense reporting forms and guidelines for how to report expenses. This is uniform for all employees. They complete the forms and abide by policy with little complaint. If there were no policy and standard form and they were questioned individually by the managers, they would take that as offensive micromanaging. People thrive with goals, guidelines, and procedures rather than with constant one-on-one oversight.

Organizations are sustained when people are empowered. If operations are based on the owners/founders being there, what happens when they are gone? What happens when they get sick? What happens when they are ready to retire? What happens when they pass away? The answer is obvious. The organization can't continue to function unless somebody like them takes over and carries on. Often, in small businesses, this is passed on to the children, who may not have the temperament or skill set to pull it off, and the business suffers. When the business suffers or fails, it can be bad for the employees. Good employees can work diligently for a long time and find themselves out of a job in small organizations with no "go forward" plan.

People who are empowered but accountable will be an asset to your organization. Those not empowered or willing to be held accountable *will* be a headache.

PEOPLE

Chapter 3

SECURITY

> **Thought:**
> How much more committed and productive would your people be if they truly felt secure?

The eternal God is your refuge . . .
Deuteronomy 33:27 (NIV)

A lot of organizations limit their understandings of employees' security to the retirement, healthcare, and other benefits portions of the total compensation package. For way too much of my career, I did not understand the depth of the security issue. It includes retirement benefits, healthcare, and other perks, but it goes deeper. The deeper aspects for people are:

- How secure are employees in their job?

- How secure are they in their relationship with you as their leader?
- Do they know where they stand with you?
- Do they believe you are for them?
- Do they believe you have their back?

Call from an Old Friend

I once got a call from a friend who had not worked for me for a long time. She was getting a new boss and was really nervous. She was putting a lot of pressure on herself trying to ensure she had the perfect first day. She wanted me to help her think of anything she may have forgotten. She told me what she had done to prepare, which was more than adequate. So, did I rack my brain trying to think of anything else she could have done? No, she was already very prepared. What she needed was not a longer list of prepared items. She needed confidence. She needed a sense of security.

So what did I do? I gave her confidence and security. I reminded her that she was the best person in her role that I knew from a very long career. I reminded her of the background the new leader was coming from and that she was better than what he'd been used to. I told her that if there was anything else he wanted, she would be more qualified to get it quickly than anyone else. By the time I finished explaining to her the confidence I had in her and how well-prepared she was, she was very calm and settled. Had I simply added to her list, she would have been even more prepared but still anxious and insecure. People are more creative and do a better job when they are calm and secure. They make mistakes when they are nervous and scared.

Sometimes, when employees ask if there's anything else they can do for you, they are not always seeking more work. Often they are seeking affirmation and security. If you have hired good employees, you have put yourself in the perfect position to be affirming from the heart when employees feel insecure. And it is crucial in affirming employees that you be genuine. The best employees can spot a fake affirmation from a long distance.

Do they believe you are for them?

To feel secure, employees need to know you are for them. You may ask who I would be for. Unfortunately, many leaders are quick to take credit for anything good and quick to place blame on employees when things don't work out. Do you really think there's security among employees under that kind of leadership?

> *"Do not look out merely for your own personal interests, but also for the interests of others."*
> *Philippians 2:4*

> *"... Give preference to one another in honor."*
> *Romans 12:10*

Unless employees simply can't pay the bills with a different job, they will leave such leaders for more security. The key here is: Do your employees believe you have their best interests in mind? Are you watching out for them? Do you really care about them? Or is your only concern the organization and perhaps yourself? When people know you are for them, they feel more secure and they are more loyal. That does not mean you are not to be a good steward of the organization's resources. It does not mean that you say employees are right when you know they are wrong. It simply means that you know you have good employees and that you are an advocate for them, keeping in balance the good of the total organization and fairness to others.

Do they believe you have their back?

I never considered myself an easy leader to work with. I tended to have high expectations of myself and others. When I left HCA, I had a great team. I really thought and feared they might be relieved to see me leave, hoping they would have an easier time with another leader. That's not what I saw as I made the transition. I sensed they considered my leaving a loss for them personally. I was curious about that. I asked them about it six months and then a year later.

I told them I knew I was not easy to work with, and I asked whether the loss they expressed was real and if so, why. Several reasons were given but the one they were all adamant about was, "Yes, you were tough, but we knew you cared about us and that you always had our back. Because you had our back, we were free to do our work without fear. We knew that you could and would take care of us." I asked them, "Isn't that what other leaders do?" They said, "Not consistently and not adamantly. We knew you would go to the mat for us." I asked all my direct reports, "And that really makes a major difference to you?" Every single person said, "Absolutely." Being a professional leader in a big organization for thirty-one years, I missed the depth of how important this issue is to people.

If you create a secure environment for people, they will tend to be loyal, dedicated, and grateful.

Chapter 4

HONOR

> **Thought:**
> How many opportunities are you missing to encourage your people through honoring them?

"Give preference to one another in honor."
Romans 12: 10

In our culture, we talk much about self-esteem. But we don't spend as much time talking about showing honor to others. We like to be thought well of. We like to be valued. It's a basic need people have. And the Bible affirms that need. It teaches us to think of others more highly than ourselves (Philippians 2:3-4). Of course, all people of all ages need to be esteemed. But I've noticed as people mature in professional life, being esteemed takes on more value.

As a practical matter, how do we do this? Really, it's quite simple. Hire people that are more gifted for their job than you are—one that they will enjoy. Then, you can appreciate their talent and their willingness to do work that you are not suited for and don't like doing.

The message of many corporate cultures, expressed or implied, is "If you can't get the job done, we will find somebody that can." This mindset doesn't place a value on past service or the value of a unique individual to the organization. It assumes that if the results aren't being achieved, it's the fault of the job holder, and a change is necessary if the results don't change. Sometimes that is the case, but often it's not.

I know people in various organizations who would trade blocks of their compensation package to be genuinely esteemed by the organization's leadership. The mistake we make in organizational life, and that I've made, is to show appreciation and esteem to people only when the results are good. We tend to show esteem most when people need it least. Think about it. People know they're doing well and feel good when the results are positive. It is when results are not positive that people need to be esteemed the most.

I remember a turnaround situation I was involved in. I was working my hardest, being the most creative, and doing some of the best work of my career. In most situations, a lot of hard work and good planning happen a long time before results turn. That's where I was. And the corporate bureaucrats, not the top leaders, constantly made life hard on me. That reminded me of the time on the family farm when I was carrying a one hundred pound feed sack, and my much smaller brother hit me at the knees. I went down, of course. You can't carry that much weight, be hit at the knees, and stay on your feet. My little brother did not know or care about that at the time. We expect better out of our leaders. But we don't always get it. I don't mean to be overly critical of others; I admit to not doing any better myself at times.

I remember vividly how it felt to be carrying such heavy weight and how unfair it felt for others to be piling on. If I had been lazy or doing the wrong thing, their involvement and follow-up could have been constructive. But since I wasn't doing anything wrong, it only took time away from important activities, caused me to work longer hours under more stress than was necessary, and with far less respect for those who were choosing to make life hard.

Chapter 4 – Honor

After many months of some of the hardest and best work I had ever done in my career, the results started to turn around. Then, people started bragging on me. They said glowing things about me. I was relieved due to the lack of pressure, but the accolades from "other people" meant nothing to me. They were not really esteeming me. They were happy over the results and giving me all the credit. I wasn't due all the credit any more than I was due all the blame earlier. When things smoothed out, I wasn't working nearly as hard, as smart, or as creatively as I was months earlier. But, I was bragged on more for my hard work and intelligence than at any other time in my career.

So what's wrong with this picture? I was doing my hardest and best work ever under constant criticism when I most needed to be esteemed and feel some sense of security. When the results changed and I felt good and secure based on the results, unneeded flattery and praise were abundant.

The situation reminds me of an interview with Jeff Fisher, who was coach of the Tennessee Titans football team. Two years earlier, the Titans had come up one yard short of winning the Super Bowl. This particular year, they were having a tough season, and the TV broadcasters and fans were giving Coach Fisher a hard time. He stared into the camera and simply said, "Listen, two years ago, we came up one yard short of winning the Super Bowl. We haven't forgotten how to coach." In the experience I described earlier, I had worked for the company for over seventeen years. It wasn't like they didn't know me, my capabilities, or my past contributions. The bureaucrats (not the top leaders) who unleashed on me simply didn't care.

I have to admit that even after that experience, I found myself doing the same thing to others at times. When we are under pressure and trying to get things done and when we are focused on our own image and reputation, it's easy to forget what other people need. Our default mode is to tell people what we want and expect, and to blame them when the results aren't there. We have to think about what other people need most in the circumstances. Often that requires us to do something or say something the opposite of what we feel like saying at the time. I'm not suggesting that you ever lie or mislead people about what you are thinking. I'm simply suggesting that sometimes we need to think more clearly. We give people an assignment because we think they can do it based on their past. If they truly can't do it, we are most at fault for delegating it to them and should point the finger at ourselves first.

If we've done a good job delegating, we should believe in the people to whom we gave the assignment, give them reasonable freedom, and follow-up at reasonable intervals. Most importantly, when the assignment is really challenging we should remember to encourage them and show our esteem for them as valuable members of the team.

THE PASTOR'S WIFE

All people need to be esteemed. Their role in life doesn't eliminate the need. It's pretty surprising, at times, the people who don't receive the esteem they should from others. I know a story about a pastor's wife who had a birthday party. She and her husband had served faithfully in ministry their whole lives. They had served one church for twenty years. The lady was a widow and some church friends were throwing her an 80th birthday party. She happened to comment how much she appreciated the party. Her next comment wasn't stated negatively but was quite a surprise. She said she had never had a party or recognition just for her. Everything else in her life had been associated with her pastor husband or the church. She was genuinely touched because at eighty years old, her church friends had a birthday party just for her.

GIZMO

Gizmo worked at the rock quarry. He wore steel-toe boots, a hard hat, and dusty clothes like everyone else who worked there. Every year, we had a Christmas barbecue lunch at the quarry. Everyone else wore their steel-toe boots, hard hats, and dusty clothes, but not Gizmo. Gizmo wore a suit and tie. As a college kid observing this for the first time, it struck me as really odd. So I asked the foreman, "What's the deal with Gizmo?" He told me that one year Gizmo dressed up a little bit for the lunch. Jim, the manager of the rock quarry, bragged on him and commented on how good he looked. Every year since then, Gizmo put on a suit and tie for the Christmas barbecue. Gizmo needed to feel important. He needed to stand out. He very deeply needed to be esteemed. The comments he got at the Christmas lunch may have been the most significant time during the year when he felt esteemed.

GOOD WAYS TO HONOR OTHERS

One of the most impactful ways of showing esteem is to write a personal note or letter. It doesn't have to be long, but it needs to be sincere, personal, and specific to the person. I remember a guy who worked for me for several years and moved twice in the process. I wrote him a personal handwritten letter thanking him for some specific contributions to the company. Years later, he talked about the letter in front of a group of people. He teared up as he said it was the first letter he ever received in his life thanking him for anything. The tragedy is he was in his mid to late 50s when I wrote the letter.

Have you ever thrown away a heartfelt note that showed you esteem?

I've seen two different men tear up from something I wrote. The first was when I was a young manager and had written a curt note on a report from an employee. I happened to walk by his office as he was reading the note and saw the hurt on his face. That was over thirty years ago. It was the first time I had ever written a note like that, and it was the last. I never wanted to be responsible for making someone feel that way again. The second man I saw tear up over something I wrote was the one I wrote the nice note to. When I saw that, I thought about how many years I had been a leader and how many opportunities I had missed to show esteem to others or to bring them joy.

Think about it. How many personal notes have you received in your life where someone showed you esteem? How many of them have you thrown away? I've never thrown any of mine away and don't plan to. That's the difference they make. It may be one of the easiest, yet most highly impactful things leaders can do.

People who do not feel valued tend to cause problems at some point. How are you honoring and esteeming people?

PEOPLE

Chapter 5

FRIENDS

> **Thought:**
> Does your team really like each other?
> Have you considered the potential
> you may be losing if they don't?

*A friend loves at all times,
and a brother is born for a time of adversity.*

Proverbs 17:17 (NIV)

We are social creatures. We were designed for relationships with others. I long ago realized that relationships are important, but being more task-oriented I likely underestimated the value of relationships in organizational life. Plus, I underestimated the role they play in bringing joy to life when given the right focus. A lawyer once asked Jesus to sum up the teachings of the Old Testament. The answer was, "Love the Lord your God with all your heart, and with all your soul, and with all your mind; and, love your neighbor as yourself." (Luke 10:27). Human beings quite simply were designed for relationships with God and others. Yes, some people are quiet and even withdrawn. That doesn't mean they don't need relationships. In fact, sometimes people with these personality profiles make the most loyal friends.

This point is proven by major firms who do employee attitude surveys for companies. A question that shows up in all the best surveys is "Do you have a best friend at work?" The surveys ask this question because it is a well-established fact that when people have a best friend at work, they are much happier and less likely to leave than those who answer no to this question. People who work together and have fun together want to stay together. Some leaders think "nose to the grindstone" teams are the most productive. I have never seen that to be true. The most productive teams are those who work together, play together, and enjoy each other's company. There's greater trust among the team members, which relates to people's need for security. It's very hard to optimize the output of the team without high levels of trust. When people know each other personally and have fun together, trust tends to grow naturally.

When I left HCA to form Vision Leadership Foundation, the thing I missed most, and without a close second, was the relationships I had with people. That's something I knew I would miss. But frankly, I didn't fully realize how much of my social life and friendships were tied to HCA. I didn't socialize outside of work with these people. My sense of professional boundaries and decorum kept me from doing that. But I was surprised to realize just how much fun, social interaction, and friendship had been built over the years.

Organizations that provide forums for employees to have fun together, socialize, and develop deeper friendships will retain people longer. They will have higher morale and, in the long-term, be more productive if the other aspects of leadership are done well.

Chapter 6

COMPENSATION

> Thought:
> Are your people more worried about their pay or their work?

*The Lord detests dishonest scales,
but accurate weights find favor with him.*

Proverbs 11:1 (NIV)

Early in my career, I made mistakes in this area. I interviewed a lot of young accountants for positions in the internal audit department. My approach was to sell them on the wonderful career opportunities available for them over the long run in such great company. We offered competitive salaries. When someone wanted to haggle over $1000 or $2000 in salary, I would get very frustrated because I thought they were missing the bigger picture of the opportunities ahead. I'm embarrassed to admit that sometimes I didn't hire really good candidates because of this frustration.

I finally realized that it didn't matter to the candidate as much what the future was until they were comfortable and could pay for their apartment, car, food, and clothing. My perspective changed. If another $1000 or $2000 really made a difference to them, was still in the pay range, and I thought they were worth it, I would hire them and tell them I expected them to earn what we were paying.

Lisa

I hired Lisa just a few years after she graduated from college. Twenty-five years later, we were having lunch introducing our daughters who were attending the same college. Lisa thanked me for hiring her. My response was that I should be thanking her because she was such a good employee and helped enormously in every position I ever put her in.

She reminded me of our first interview. She wanted $2000 more than I initially offered. I thought she was an outstanding candidate and quickly gave her the $2000 and finalized the offer. I told her I expected she would earn the extra money. Her first project was rather complicated, and she did an outstanding job. Within six months, we paid a special one-time bonus to everyone on the team including Lisa for their good work. The $2000 and extra bonus cost very little from the company's perspective, but we got a truly outstanding employee who worked for the company for many years and in several positions. I shudder to think of the lost opportunities for the company if I had been shortsighted in this situation over the starting salary.

This doesn't mean that I paid all candidates what they asked for in an interview. I only did that for truly outstanding candidates who were in entry level positions.

Chapter 7

DIRECTION, CONNECTION, AND CONTEXT

> **Thought:**
> How much easier would it be to lead and guide your organization if everyone agreed with the mission and were excited about the vision? Do your people even know the mission and vision of your organization? Do they know where they fit in?

"Come, let us rebuild the wall of Jerusalem..."
Nehemiah 2:17

People need to feel connected to a purpose larger than themselves. "Hire people who are mission driven. This is why Steve Jobs was so successful."[6] That's one of many reasons why so many people wanted to work for HCA. They felt they were part of something really significant. Leaders need to help those under them see their purpose in the organization. People need to understand where they fit in and how they impact the organization. They also want to know where the organization is going.

How do you know if the mission and vision of your organization is clear? How do you know if you've done enough to rightly connect people to the organization's mission and vision?

Giving people clear direction, connection, and context requires clear understanding and communication of the items below:

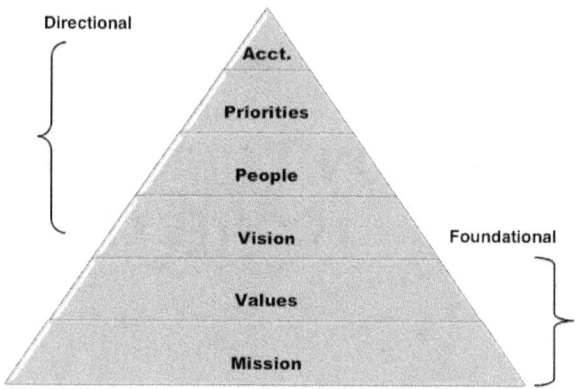

I. Mission

The mission describes why the organization exists.[7] It deals with questions like "Why are we here?" "Why do we exist?" and "Why do we get up each day and do what we do?"[8] Mission is about purpose, and it draws people who want to align with that purpose.[9]

II. Values

Values clarify what you stand for and believe in.[10] Values are guiding principles that influence both "who and what fit in around here."[11] Values need to be clearly stated. But, most importantly, they have to be lived out in day-to-day life by the leader. I've seen the power of positive values lived out and the destructive nature of stated values not lived out. Studies have shown that people stay with organizations for less money and other perks if their values are aligned. People are either drawn to the values of an organization or leave because of them. Values are foundational to the organization and once established should not change over time. Some people teach and write about values as though they are directional. I see values as more foundational. They are something you can build an organization on or something that can cause one to crumble. Core values are the principles and standards at the very center of our character.[12]

III. Vision

"Truly great organizations are crystal clear about where they are going."[13] Proverbs 29:18 (KJV) says, "Where there is no vision, the people perish." Without vision, there is no hope for the future or sense of direction. When people lose hope, there are no goals or dreams.

"While mission is a statement of what is, a vision is a statement of what or how you would like things to be—a picture of the future you're working to create. Nothing was ever created without vision."[14]

"A vision statement is the other side of the coin of a mission statement. It is a picture of a mission fulfilled. Whereas mission speaks to the head for decision, vision speaks to the heart for inspiration. 'Can you imagine if...'"[15]

> Goals can be energizing-when you win.
> But a vision is more powerful than a goal.
> A vision is enlivening, it's spirit-giving,
> it's the guiding force behind all great
> human endeavors.
> Vision is about shared energy, a sense of awe,
> a sense of possibility. [16]
>
> Benjamin Zander, Conductor
> Boston Philharmonic Orchestra

IV. People

Staffing an organization with people who agree with the mission, believe in the values, are excited about the vision, understand the priorities, and accept accountability is critical to a successful organization. What is expected of the people and their ability to work with the team are critical components to success. Individuals must accept and be accountable for goals that will help the organization achieve its mission and vision.

Each individual needs to know how they fit into the triangle and how they contribute meaningfully.

V. Priorities

Priorities help an organization and people focus. They save time and resources while building momentum and strength. They are expressed through strategies, tactics, goals, and objectives. Peter Drucker says, "Objectives must be derived from what our business (organization) is, what it will be, and what it should be."[17]

VI. Accountability

When God created the world, He gave people great freedom, but with accountability. Adam and Eve were given dominion over every living thing with only one restriction—the tree of the knowledge of good and evil. (Genesis 2:15-17). And there was a consequence associated with violating that one restriction which they unfortunately experienced. The Bible has much to say about accountability. It is a twofold concept including the promise of reward and potential for discipline or correction. This is illustrated many times in the lives of God's people in the Old Testament. Deuteronomy 28 outlines the blessings of God for following Him and the curses for ignoring Him. Accountability is often thought of in a negative sense. However, biblical accountability should generally be thought of in a positive sense. God told Cain, "If you do well, will not your countenance be lifted up?"(Genesis 4:7). The restrictions are for your benefit, and any discipline you receive is to bring you back onto the right path. For example, King David said in Psalm 119:71, "It is good for me that I was afflicted, that I may learn your statutes." Scripture says that those whom God loves He rebukes and chastens as a father who loves his son (Proverbs 3:11-12; Hebrews 12:3-11).

> **Summary**
>
> 1. **Mission** gives people purpose.
> 2. **Values** give them a foundation to depend on and a behavioral framework to operate within.
> 3. **Vision** gives hope and direction.
> 4. **People** attracted to the mission and vision can be trusted with a piece of the vision.
> 5. **Priorities** give focus and a feeling of importance.
> 6. **Accountability** gives people encouragement to do their best.

God is a God of order, not of chaos. People need structure and they need context to know where they fit in. Whether you are interviewing a new employee or volunteer, or dealing with an existing one, you can ask a lot of open-ended questions such as the following: What about our mission and vision excite you? Which of our values resonate with you most and least? Do you think we have the right priorities established? Do you feel like what we are asking of you fits with your talents and passion? Do we have you in your sweet spot? Do you think the accountability system is fair?

Connecting the team with the mission, vision, and values of the organization is key.

People who agree with your mission, are attracted by your values, agree with your vision and priorities, are well suited for their role, and agree to be held accountable for a portion of the priorities will be an asset. Those who don't will be a *headache*.

CATHEDRAL

So what is the practical thing we must do regularly for leaders to create that sense of connection? Perhaps the answer is best illustrated in the story of the cathedral.

PEOPLE

A man noticed three brick layers who appeared to be doing exactly the same thing. He walked up to the first one and said, "May I ask what you are doing?" The man replied, "I am a brick layer. I lay bricks on top of each other all day long and get paid $15 an hour to feed my family. It's hard work."

The gentleman asked the second man the same question. He replied, "I'm a builder. I love building. And it lets me feed my family."

The gentleman went to the third man with the same question. The man replied, "Oh sir, I'm building a great cathedral. I love building. But this building is special. It will be grand and beautiful. Many people will gather here to worship. Their spiritual lives and destinies will be changed in this mighty cathedral. I'm so blessed to have the opportunity to be part of this project. Can you believe it? I get to participate in something so special and actually be paid for it." [18]

The point is that all three men were performing the same activity, on the same project, and for the same pay. But they had radically different perspectives.

The first one could only see the task he performed as a duty because of what he and his family got out of it. It felt like labor and drudgery to him. He is like those individuals in the organization who are given a task to do with no explanation or connection to how it fits into what the organization is doing.

The second man had a broader perspective. He saw himself as a builder. He enjoyed his work and was thankful that he got paid. Unlike the other person, he was exercising his natural talents and passion in his work. He is like those individuals who enjoy being part of the organization they are with, but they are not connected mentally and emotionally to the mission and vision of the organization.

The third man saw the uniqueness of what he was building and felt truly fortunate to be part of it. He was grateful that he could be part of something so grand and, on top of that, get paid to support his family. This man was connected to the mission and vision of what he was doing. He saw the work as a privilege of being part of something bigger than himself. He is like those individuals who are committed to the mission and vision of an organization. They are using their natural talents. The mission and vision resonates with their passions. They sense they are fulfilling their destiny or calling in life. If they didn't need money to live, they would do the same thing and work just as hard at it.

Isn't this what we see in all kinds of organizations, regardless of the type of work performed? Some see their job as only the task, the labor, and the drudgery for which they get paid. Some see their work as what they do, enjoy it, and are glad they get paid. Some see their work as part of something great and feel privileged to be part of it. And at times, they are amazed they get paid for doing something so wonderful.

What are the key differences? One is people doing what they are most talented at and having a passion and sense of purpose for doing it. The other is having more information and a broader perspective of what they are part of. The leader impacts both of these by:

- Putting people in roles for which they have the talent, passion, and "calling;"
- Empowering them to carry out those roles;
- Supporting them when they need help; and
- Sharing information and perspective about how what they do fits with the mission and vision of the organization in a meaningful way. This requires ongoing communication with the team.

EXAMPLE

I know a person who is a great executive assistant. She worked for a demanding executive for several years. After he left his role, I thought she would be relieved because he was so demanding and she worked so hard. After a few months, but before his position was filled, I asked her if she was happier. She said, "No, not at all." I asked her, "Aren't you working less?" She replied, "Yes." I asked, "Then, why aren't you happier?"

She said, "I did work really hard when he was here. But, he would tell me what we were doing and why. I felt like I was contributing in a meaningful way to what was happening in the company. Now I feel like I'm pushing paper, taking calls, and scheduling." In other words, she was really saying she went from feeling like a cathedral builder to feeling like a brick layer. Unfortunately, organizations do this to people frequently.

That discussion really struck me. We change people's perspective when we explain their jobs/roles and share other pertinent information in the light of the organizational mission and vision. It gives purpose to what we are doing. It's like the difference between a brick layer and a person building a great cathedral. This sharing of information and perspective is something that should happen all the time in a healthy organization.

> **"Cathedral Builders" tend to be an organization's greatest asset. Builders are also assets. Brick layers become brick throwers and usually the biggest headache of leadership.**

Chapter 8

CLEAR PRIORITIES

> Thought:
> How much time are you wasting and how much extra stress are you enduring because you're not focused on priorities?

"The way is narrow that leads to life."
Matthew 7:14

People are not good at establishing and sticking to priorities. How do I know? Nearly everyone I know is too busy!

Everywhere I go, it seems executives keep getting busier. There aren't enough hours in the day. The work backlogs get bigger, and the stress seems to increase. I understand. My life has felt this way many times. But we need to understand the concept of "less is more."

THE RIVER

Picture in your mind's eye a river. The river is two miles wide and has barges and boats and dinghies on it. They are spaced a safe distance apart with each carrying cargo. A certain amount of goods can be moved in a day's time on this river, even without any other power source, because it is flowing at five miles per hour. If you wanted to move the most goods down the river in the least amount of time, what would you do?

Let's assume you had the ability to narrow the banks of the river. Now instead of being two miles wide, it's a mile wide and flowing at ten miles per hour. For this to be safe, you have to take the sailboats and dinghies off the river and all you'll have left are the barges. In this scenario, would you be able to move more goods in less time? Of course you would.

Now, let's think about any area of your life and see if this isn't also true. Let us take work for an example. Let's compare the width of the river to the breadth of the project lists and activities you have. As leaders, we have many choices to narrow the number of activities we engage in and the number of projects we pursue. Now let's compare the barges to those projects and activities that really "move the needle," as the leadership used to say at HCA. We had some very savvy operators who were highly focused, not on small items but on those things that had the greatest impact. When you see boats on the river, especially sailboats, they normally have a name on them. They appeal to our pride, and they are flashy and fast compared to a barge. Let's compare the boats in organizational life to those projects or initiatives that have particular individuals' thumbprints on them. It is a matter of pride to them. These are smaller projects that can move quickly, but over time they don't do much to "move the needle." The only sailboat-type projects that should be left in place are those that have the potential for barge-type impact later.

Now let's compare the dinghies in organizational life to those pet projects of the leader. These are small blips on the radar screen, and the leader can control them, but they do nothing to "move the needle." These things in organizational life still take administrative time and effort to follow up on, and they take some resources. I have seen many times in a big company that when the focus is narrowed to the big projects that really move the needle, more progress is made in a shorter period of time. We see this in the Bible in the book of Nehemiah. The Great Wall of Jerusalem was rebuilt in fifty-two days (Nehemiah 6:15), a task thought unachievable. How did this happen? It was the single focus of all the people, and they did more than they thought possible during that timeframe.

Most books on time management have a number of tricks and techniques that are useful in helping you be more efficient with your time. But I know through experience that narrowing my focus and concentrating on the high-potential projects always yields the best results.

COMMON MISTAKES

Mistake # 1 – Unclear priorities

I remember when I assumed responsibility for a new corporate department trying to assess the department's priorities. It quickly became clear there was no true sense of priorities there. Those in the department were simply trying to make the operators they were dealing with at the time happy. Naturally, there was much wasted activity. Substantial money was being spent on plans and projects that had no hope of being approved. There was much other wasted activity with no sense of direction. Some of the activity even worked against the company in the long run.

> *"Let all things be done decently and in order."*
> *1 Corinthians 14:40 (KJV)*

I led the team to assess strengths, weaknesses, opportunities, and future threats. From that analysis, we put together a set of goals and priorities and had them endorsed by senior management. The team saved millions of dollars and did a better job for the company with much less stress and anxiety because they had clear priorities.

How did we save so much money? We did it by having a process through which we sought approval of senior management before spending substantial money on projects that would eventually be rejected. How did we do a better job for the company? We did it by having everyone focus on high-priority projects that would make a difference and would be approved. How did we reduce stress and anxiety for the team? Prior to this process, everyone in the department had the stress of keeping each individual operator happy. The corporate team had the stress of realizing that sometimes what operators wanted and what was best for the company were at odds. But, they felt they would ultimately get evaluated based on keeping each individual operator happy. When the new process was implemented, it was senior management making the decisions on project priorities before a great deal of money and time was spent on weak projects. The people in the corporate department were not "pitted" against the operators in the field. The operations satisfaction ratings of this department went up. The team had much greater satisfaction and less stress. They spent time on high-impact projects. They were not chasing projects and spending time that would ultimately be wasted while stretching those involved too thin. Eliminating unproductive work and enabling people to make progress on things that "move the needle" blesses the people.

It is not uncommon in large companies for people in support areas to work really hard to make whomever they're dealing with happy but with no real sense of priority for the greater good of the organization. Specifically, non-profit organizations frequently experience mission creep which in turn leads to the blurring of priorities.

Mistake # 2 – Too many priorities

One of my group vice presidents came back from a division president's meeting one time and was quite excited about the priorities the division president presented. I looked at the sheet and quickly said, "Problem." He looked at me astonished and asked what was wrong with the priorities. He asked me which ones I didn't like. I said, "Each of them is fine. The problem is there are twelve of them. Can people focus clearly on twelve different things?" My experience has shown if you go beyond five to seven objectives/priorities for an annual cycle you start diluting the effort, and people lose focus.

> **News Flash, Leaders!**
> **If you have a bunch of them,**
> **they aren't all real priorities.**

So, how does focusing on priorities in your organization bless people? It brings simplicity to complexity. It makes sure people are pulling together toward the key priorities resulting in greater accomplishment and satisfaction for them and the whole team. It assures the leader and employees are on the same page, resulting in fewer expectation gaps, conflicts, and instances of confusion.

Chapter 8 – Clear Priorities

Let's think about how a river works. The more the river banks narrow, the deeper the channel gets, and the faster and stronger the water flows. Priorities in organizations act like river banks. Initiatives flow faster and stronger. Priorities create "tipping points" in organizations like the great waterfall on a river. Things move with great speed, and a powerful, almost unstoppable force is created. It has great power and a certain beauty about it.

One time I was consulting with a large church that was getting ready to double in membership. In working with the staff, I tried to assess the priorities. In a team meeting, I asked people to share their priorities. The chief administrative leader had a page of activities front and back. I said, "I think that's too much for you to get done. What are your top three priorities?" He lifted his hands with a bewildered look and said, "I have no idea." If the lead administrative person has more than they can do and no sense of priority, what do you think it was like for the team? There was chaos, confusion, and anxiety among them. In fact, if things proceeded on the present course, I perceived it was only a matter of time until high turnover would occur. Even though this was a church, I hardly saw it as an environment where employees were being blessed. Here's the point. This leader and the whole team were really good people. The church was a good church. Everybody had good intentions. People worked hard and did their best. But with lack of clear priorities, anxiety, chaos, and confusion were rampant in the lives of these people.

Mistake # 3 – Favoring good over best

The leader's job in today's world can seem a lot like farming. The work never seems to get done. There never seems to be enough time. Leaders are often driven individuals who lean toward being competitive workaholics. Therefore, their solution is to work longer hours and require others to work longer hours. This goes on until higher and higher turnover results. Then, the leader may eventually experience burnout.

Sometimes enterprising leaders say, "We need to be more efficient." They may read time management books for the latest ideas on efficiency. They may call on their team to come up with efficiency ideas. This is what my internal audit team did when I challenged them to cut the length of the workday to reduce turnover. Many times organizations can be more efficient. But this begs the question, "Is it more important to be efficient or effective?"

When I led the internal audit department, it was not uncommon for teams to work until eight or nine o'clock at night, have dinner, and then work more in their hotel rooms. Needless to say, we had high turnover. People left on average after six months to one year. It seemed we were always hiring, always training new people, and always trying to do complicated work with inexperienced people.

I noticed that these late nights were the norm with some supervisors while other supervisors completed their audits with more normal hours. After much discussion with the leadership team about employing efficiency techniques, we went the route of looking at effectiveness issues and priorities. Auditors like to dot every "i" and cross every "t." But not all work in any audit is of equal value. We started talking about working smarter, not harder. This meant that we would have to determine what truly was high priority work. We prioritized the steps that were mission-critical. We never compromised on those. We held open the option of changing the scope of the audit depending on the time available. With that change, we were able to make the schedules reasonable and retain people for much longer, resulting in higher qualified people doing better audit work.

The same thing happened years later when I was responsible for the Physician Services department. This was a function with substantial responsibilities and a good deal of complexity. I really thought I was managing my time well and was highly focused on only the most important priorities. Then, I had a major surgery. I had to transition back into work first two hours a day, then four, then six, and then finally a regular schedule. I discovered that I could do all my high-priority work in two to four hours a day. The rest of the time was really spent on lesser priorities, meetings, miscellaneous administrative tasks, and bureaucratic activities that I got a "pass" on during this time.

Chapter 9

BALANCED PRIORITIES

> **Thought:**
> Have you ever considered how much stronger your organization could be in the long term if you helped your team be more balanced?

"Do not merely look out for your own personal interests, but also for the interests of others."

Philippians 2:4

PEOPLE NEED BALANCE

Talking about balanced priorities may seem to contradict what we said in the previous chapter about the need to narrow our focus. And I do believe it is true that we might "accomplish" more by a narrower focus. However, this is not generally healthy, and most people would not be happy.

Life is like a wheel on a car.[19] If it gets out of balance, it feels lonely and uncomfortable. Most people I know feel their lives don't have the balance they want.

Sometimes leaders think the organization can't be successful if employees are encouraged or allowed to give significant priority to other goals in life. I'm reminded of the story of the hare and the tortoise. The tortoise won the race instead of the expected winner, the hare. It's been my experience that people who are very conscious of the choices they make and feel good about the balance they have based on their "calling" in life actually contribute more to the organization and accomplish the most in every area of their lives.

I remember a movie about a dogsled race. The team that took periodic rests actually beat the teams that kept going all the time. This is the principle of observing the Sabbath day. People can get more done by resting every seventh day than by continuing to work all the time.

It is sometimes surprising to see what people will give up in life to achieve a particular goal or complete a project at their job. Often people make significant trade-offs for projects they won't remember a year later. I remember many times almost insisting that employees take time off to be with sick parents or to be at some significant event for their children. These were cases where I'm really convinced they would not have done it without my encouragement. I was impressed by their dedication but marveled at their lack of insight regarding the true priorities in life. I say that remembering some poor decisions I made myself, especially early in my career. I wish I could go back to make more holistic and conscious decisions about what matters most in life.

Jesus never seemed in a hurry. He was stressed at times, but it didn't come from a full schedule, too much to do, and worry over not getting everything done on His "to do" list. His earthly ministry was three years, and on the cross He said, "It is finished." He completed all the work that He was assigned to do. Yet, Jesus had balance. I'm told that the checkerboard square, which is a brand symbol of the Ralston Purina Corporation, was created by the founder to show the balance in Jesus' life.

Luke 2:52 says, "And Jesus increased in wisdom and stature, and in favor with God and man." In other words, Jesus grew mentally and emotionally, physically, spiritually, and socially. Jesus had goals and spent time in the four balanced areas of life. Yet, He did so without anxiety and stress over a busy schedule.

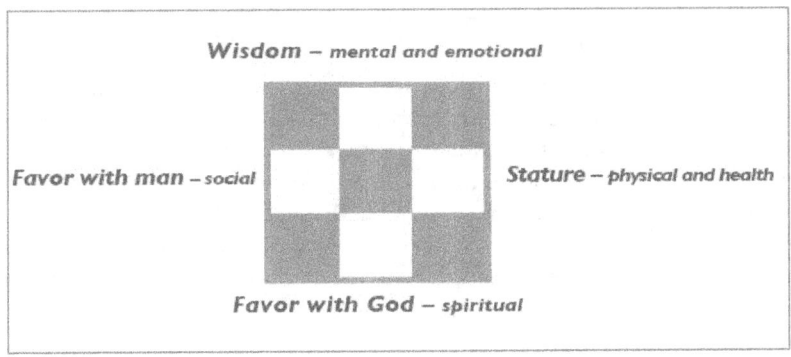

I once interviewed what appeared to be a bright, aggressive young man. I remember asking him where he wanted to be in ten years. He said he wanted to be sitting in my chair. I said that was great because I had other goals, and I wanted to be sitting in another chair by then anyway.

Later, I offered him a job, which he promptly turned down. I asked him why. He responded that he had a dog and that he could not be out of town and leave his dog that much. I told him I respected his concern for his dog, and there's nothing wrong with being that attached to a pet. I did, however, go on to explain to him that he had an important decision to make. I explained that he had lofty goals he would never achieve if his goal of being at home with his dog took priority. I reminded him of saying his goal was to sit in my chair in ten years. I explained that sitting in my chair or one like it would require some changes in his priorities.

Striking a healthy balance is something that people seem to struggle with. Leaders are in a position to make the struggle harder or easier for people. We can help them or hurt them in the process. If we are going to bless people, that means we should help them.

A PRIORITY-DRIVEN LIFE NARROWS THE FOCUS

People, especially leaders, are the busiest I have ever seen them. Leaders want more time, more freedom, and less stress. How is that even possible in organizational life today? The key is how you approach life. Are you going through life like a rifle bullet or like a shotgun blast? Let me explain. A rifle bullet is much smaller than the shotgun shell. It has less powder and less lead. It takes less powder because there's only one piece of small lead at the end as it leaves the barrel moving straight toward its target. It takes less powder to propel the smaller piece of lead a great distance. By contrast, a shotgun shell has much more powder and more lead. The lead is a bunch of pellets, called buckshot. They look like small BBs. They come out of the shotgun barrel and scatter, hitting a bigger target area. The shooter can be less accurate with a shotgun and still hit the target. Since the buckshot scatters and is small, it doesn't go nearly as far as a rifle bullet.

This analogy is like some people's lives. Some people are highly focused on a singular objective or a limited number of objectives, and they can go far. Other people's lives have so many activities that they are more like a shotgun blast. They cover a lot of territory but don't make as much progress as the person who is more focused.

Jesus modeled a life that had three critical components. First, He had balance. Second, He had a clear purpose. And, third, He was extremely focused on a narrower set of goals than most people believed He should pursue.

People without clear priorities lose their effectiveness and value.
People with too many priorities may cause headaches for leadership.

Part II

HOW THE LEADER GETS WHAT THE ORGANIZATION NEEDS FROM PEOPLE

If you had an organization that depended upon high-tech equipment for results, you would like to know as much about the equipment as possible. You would need to know when the equipment got obsolete. You would need to know how to treat the equipment to get the best results. You would need to follow the instructions in operating the equipment.

In the same vein, you need to know your people, understand their unique personalities, and engage the right people for the right job.

Just like equipment can become obsolete, jobs can outgrow people so that they no longer fit.

You need to know how to help underperformers and influence motivation positively. You need to create a culture that empowers.

PEOPLE

Progress requires leading positive change. Documentation and training become more necessary as organizations expand. So do enabling control systems.

Finally, progress has to be measured and shared with the team. Measuring what matters most and sharing the results is important in leading teams to the next level.

It's possible that you are good at giving people what they need. You still have to be good at getting what the organization needs from them. Otherwise, they feel like a burden, not an asset.

Chapter 10

KNOW YOUR PEOPLE

> **Thought:**
> Have you ever considered how strong your organization would be if people there clearly understood their calling (purpose) and their unique talents, and they could contribute directly to the mission/vision of the organization by pursuing their calling and using their unique talents?

"For I know the plans that I have for you, declares the Lord, plans for welfare and not for calamity to give you a future and hope."

Jeremiah 29:11

There is a reason why the old TV show *Cheers* resonated so much with people. It was expressed in their theme song, "You want to go where everybody knows your name." People want to be known and understood.

God has great plans for us. If we cooperate with Him, He carries out these plans in our lives because He knows us better than we know ourselves. God put trout in mountain streams because that's where they fit. He put marlin in the ocean because that's where they belong. Not all fish are the same. They do not prosper and survive in just any environment. Likewise, individuals don't just prosper and survive anywhere. They do best in the environment they were created for.

A lawyer once asked Jesus to sum up all of the teachings of Scripture up to that point. Jesus told the lawyer, in essence, to love God with all his being and his neighbor as himself. When you lead an organization, how do you love your neighbor as yourself when you're hiring people or making assignments? If you're going to bless people through your organization, there are five things you have to be aware of in hiring and in ongoing delegation:

- **Purpose**, which I refer to as people's callings. What did God create them to do and accomplish?
- **Personality profile**, which is their hardwiring and unique personality traits.
- **Passion**, which is what they care about deeply.
- **Preparation**, which includes their education, work experience, and other life experiences.
- **Potential**, which includes their ability to grow with the job and organization.

There is a difference between pursuing a *calling* and just having a job. Having the ability for something is not enough. The word vocation comes from the Latin word meaning "to call." It suggests you are listening for something that is calling out to you, listening for God's voice—something that is particular to you. A calling is something you have to listen for—a connection to something larger than yourself.[1]

Stephen Covey[2] says we all want "to live, to love, to learn and to leave a legacy." There's no better way to leave a legacy than by following our calling.

God called me to work with leaders who would grow His kingdom. The balance all of us as leaders must maintain is influencing each situation for the good of the organization and for increase in the kingdom of God.

It is easy to assume that because people have similar personality profiles—hardwiring—they are the same. There will be some similarities, habits, and approaches to work, but that doesn't mean they're the same.

Our *talents* are different. People with similar profiles can have different talents. There are a lot of people with profiles similar to mine that are a lot smarter than I am. Scripture says God gave one man one talent, another man two talents, and another man five talents. We are accountable to use our talents, but we all have different talents. (The word *talent* is applicable in the investing and use of both money and God-given gifts and abilities.)

Our *experiences* differ. I led the internal audit department in a big corporation for a number of years. My personality profile may be very similar to others in the company with similar roles. But I grew up on a very small dairy farm in western Kentucky, and the work experiences I had are significantly different from those of others. They had and always will have an impact on my mind, emotions, and spirit. I may respond very differently in certain situations than anybody else would because of my experiences.

Our *passions* differ. I am familiar with an executive at a large hospital in the role of Chief Quality Officer. All hospitals have a similar type role, but this particular executive is special. She lost her son because of a clinical error that should have never happened. I expect that she approaches her job with dedication, zeal and quality well above and beyond people who have not had a similar experience.

I believe people are unique. In our culture, we like to rate people as average, above average, or below average. This starts in grade school with the bell-shaped curve for grading people and continues throughout our lives. People may be average, above average, or below average in the use of their talents, but they are all unique. The combination of their personality profiles, talents, experiences, passions, and callings makes them different from anyone else ever created. Scientists tell us no two snowflakes are identical. Do you think God ran out of ideas on people?

Mistakes

I always made mistakes when I only looked at a person through a limited lens. Businesses tend to look primarily at preparation and experience while ministries tend to look more at calling and educational preparation. Let's look at these in more detail.

Looking only at preparation and experience

Let's understand how these interrelate and identify common mistakes leaders make in this very important area. In most businesses, there is an over concentration on preparation. Employers want to know that people have the skill and experience to do the job. They also want people who want a job, but they often are not careful to assess whether these people have passion for the job or if they just need and want the job for the income.

Most managers (vs. leaders) hire and assign work based on talent and experience only. But I believe every person was created for a unique purpose in the universe and in God's kingdom. The mentality in many organizations is that "if you can't get it done, I will find somebody that will." The truth is that if a job is not getting done, a change very well may be in order. But all individuals are unique and if they are the right people for the job, nobody else can do it exactly like they can—they should be treated as such.

As a Christian leader, if your main concern is finding somebody that has the skill and experience to do a job, but doing it is not consistent with their God given "calling," or they do not have great passion for the job, you're simply using that person and their skills for your purposes. If, however, the job you give a person is consistent with their calling, personality profile, passions, and preparation, you have a situation where neither party is using the other. Rather, the organization has meaningful work that needs to be done to serve society and engages people to do it who can live out their calling in that role, express their passion through it in a way that is consistent with their personality profile, and put into practice how God has prepared them up to this point. There is not only great harmony in this arrangement, there's also less conflict. This arrangement creates a much more productive environment and much higher morale for the entire team, allowing the leader to be a much better steward of the organization's resources.

Ignoring personality profiles

I'm thinking of at least two different people now in leadership roles. Over time, I have seen them get extremely frustrated and angry at some of their key people. As they talked out with me their frustrations and anger over the performance of their people, I began to understand the personality profiles of the people. It became very clear to me that the problem was not with the people. They were really good, hard-working people, well qualified for their primary role. The frustration and anger came in when the employers asked them to do things that they did not have the personality profile for. The employers assumed that because they were excellent at certain things, they should be able to do the other things they wanted them to do. That just wasn't the case.

One example in particular stands out. Jim was constantly irritated with the performance of Joe. I asked why he didn't just release him and be done with the aggravation. He said that Joe was really good at certain things. I asked what Joe was good at, and Jim explained. Jim also listed those things he needed but which Joe was never good at. We ran a personality profile which indicated Joe was hardwired to be good at those things where he had been successful but had no aptitude for the other list of things that Jim wanted. I asked Jim about just delegating those things to Joe he was good at and doing the rest himself or finding someone else for the other work he needed done. He did, and they have had a successful working relationship for a number of years. I must acknowledge, however, the difficulty that a person in a smaller organization with limited staff has in this area. There is always the temptation to want someone to do something beyond an individual skill set and personality profile. I had this temptation many times even in a large organization.

Ignoring passion

There are a number of business employers and some ministries and non-profits that use personality profiles in their selection process. I believe this adds to their success rate in finding people who fit the job. However, you can still have someone who has the right personality profile and the necessary preparation to do the job but still doesn't have a calling and passion for it. I know a young man trained as an accountant. He does a very effective job where he works, and his boss would be distraught if he lost him. However, the young man has no real passion for accounting, even though he's good at it. His real passion is cars. He knows everything about cars and loves working on them. He can do incredible things better than most mechanics. In the role he's in, he's being used by an employer as an accountant, but I believe his true calling and passion would have him serving people by doing a good honest job of repairing their cars. He has both the personality profile for that, as well as adequate preparation. If he followed his calling and passion, all the dots would connect for him. He makes a good living at what he's doing, but he would have a better life doing what he is called to do. And, in this circumstance, the individual would likely have a higher standard of living and more independence.

Using people versus engaging

Do you know why many leaders don't consider the whole person in making hiring or delegation decisions? I'll use my own experience as the example. Frankly, many times I was so interested in getting the job done that I used people to accomplish the task rather than looking at the world from their perspective. I wasn't trying to make sure that what I asked them to do matched their hardwiring, talents, experiences, passions, and callings. Over my career, I hired hundreds and likely well over a thousand individuals. I made thousands of job assignments. To be honest, most of the time I had in mind what I needed done and would help reach the objectives that I needed to achieve for the organization. If I had understood what God has made painfully clear to me now, I would have put even more time in the interview process and the thought process before delegating and making assignments, and I would have had an even more effective organization. I would have been a better steward of what God had entrusted to me.

The most effective organization I can imagine is one where people are hired or join the organization with a very clear sense of their calling in life. If they can clearly live out their calling and contribute directly to the mission of the organization, you have an ideal fit. In this environment, people do what they do because they feel like that's what they were created to do. There's no forcing them. While money is important because they need to make a living and provide for their family, more money won't necessarily cause them to work harder if they are living out their calling. They will work harder, be more committed, be very hesitant to ever leave the organization, and look out for the best interests of the organization if they can achieve the vision of the organization by living out their calling. In this type of culture, problems and friction are avoided. Morale and productivity are high. Customer service improves and so does profitability.

How about you? When you are hiring or making job assignments, do you consider:

- The calling of your people?
- What they are really passionate about?
- Their personality profile? Do you really think about how the job or assignment fits how they're hardwired? Or is it just something you think they should be able to do?
- Their preparation? Do you know them well enough to know what they are truly capable of so that you'll give them work to do which they're not going to fail at?
- Their potential to grow in the job and with the organization?

If you don't know your people and engage them as partners, they may be headaches rather than assets.

PEOPLE

Chapter 11

UNDERSTAND PEOPLE'S PERSONALITIES – THEIR HARDWIRING

> **Thought:**
> Have you ever wondered how much more productive and fun your work could be if you really understood what makes your people "tick"?

"For you formed my inward parts; you knitted me together in my mother's womb... intricately woven."

Psalm 139:13-15 (ESV)

More than once in my career, I've closed my door, sat down, and banged my head on the top of my desk saying, "What were you thinking?" The truth is I was really confused about what I was thinking and why I had just taken a certain action. I don't know if you've ever banged your head on your desk, but I strongly suspect you've had the same feeling as I had at some point in your life.

The truth is many leaders do not know themselves well, nor do they understand other people. What's the solution? We need to understand how we and others are made—our hardwiring or personality profile.

We seem to be schizophrenic in organizational life about our people. Most successful organizations have some value statement affirming the worth of their people, such as "people are our greatest asset." Yet some leaders complain about their teams, saying things like, "My job would be fun if it weren't for the people." The truth is, your people can bring great joy to your life and value to the organization. Or they can bring great pain, problems, and destruction in organizational life. So how do we understand ourselves and others better? One piece of this is by understanding personality profiles.

God knows us, and He knows us intimately. He knows the purpose He created us for. He knows everything we need to live out our destiny. As leaders, one of our goals should be to help our people discern their uniqueness and live out their own God-given purpose.

Every mechanic has a toolbox. Good mechanics know what every tool is to be used for and how to use it. Imagine a mechanic who did not know the difference between a 5/8 inch socket wrench, a 1 inch open-end wrench, and a monkey wrench. Do you think he could make a living? Would you want him working on your car? Of course not!

Electricians have a lot of knowledge about wiring. In fact, they are required to have a license showing their knowledge of wiring. If they do not know what they're doing, they could electrocute themselves. They could do a faulty job and burn a building down. If this happened, other people could be hurt or killed.

Assume a building contractor allows an unlicensed electrician to work on his job. The electrician does faulty wiring, the building burns, and people are killed. What happens to the building contractor? He is sued for damages to the building. He is likely sued by family members for causing death or injury to people. It's possible he could even face criminal charges. In other words, there's great accountability for letting people deal with the wiring in the building when they don't have sufficient knowledge.

How does this apply to leadership? The height of God's creation in terms of value, worth, and complexity is human beings. Among all the resources God gives leaders to work with, the most important is people. These people have unique personalities—hardwiring—that God gave them. We refer to these as personality profiles. What do most leaders understand about personality profiles in general and specifically the personality profiles of the people they are impacting? Very little! I shudder to think how little I understood about the personality profiles of people when I began leading.

Owners of businesses and leaders of other organizations give people management responsibility with significant influence over the lives of people. These appointed managers often have very little understanding of personality profiles. When you're dealing with people "hardwired" a specific way, but you have little understanding of that hardwiring, it's likely that over time you're going to fry their minds, emotions, motivations, passions, and spirits. No licenses are required for leaders and managers to understand the hardwiring of people, and there's no accountability for the owner when bad things happen.

So, how can we understand the hardwiring of our people? God knows us intimately because He made us. Jeremiah 29:6 says, "Before you were formed in your mother's womb, I knew you." We can begin to understand how people are designed by understanding and using personality profiles in our work.

UNDERSTANDING PEOPLE'S PERSONALITIES

Have you ever seen a trout in a mountain stream? They are actually hard to see unless the sunlight hits them just right or they make a sudden movement. They seem to just blend and flow with the stream. It all seems rather effortless. They just seem to fit that mountain stream, don't they? But not every fish fits a mountain stream. There are salmon that swim upstream and die after laying their eggs. Marlins don't fit a mountain stream at all. They belong in an ocean.

I remember a conversation with a guy at a key point in his career. He was trying to determine if he would take the CEO job in a big company or the CEO job in a small start-up company. After listening to him for a while, I told him that he wasn't meant, at that point in his life, to be a big fish in a small pond but rather a big fish in the ocean. That statement immediately resonated with him. How God made us determines where and what we are suited for. Understanding our unique personality profile is one step toward understanding how God made us.

So, at a very practical level, how do you give people what they need? One place to start is by understanding personality profiles. First of all, it helps you select the right people when you're hiring. Certain personality profiles go with certain jobs or roles. If you take the time to profile people before you interview them you can avoid (for both them and you) spending time looking at roles that don't fit them. You can ask better questions to discern if they are the right person for the role and therefore will be happy in it.

Also, profiling helps you in ongoing job assignments, giving people projects and initiatives that play to their strengths. And it helps your ability to improve teamwork in the organization. You understand each team member and what they need in order to relate properly. You also know how to counsel people and improve their interpersonal relationships. You know how to best communicate with your team members and how to delegate consistent with their style.

In the rest of this chapter, I will give examples of how personality profiles work in order to give you a working understanding of a basic profile and how to use this it.

There are many good systems on the market. For purposes of this discussion, we will refer to one of the oldest and most basic—the **DISC**. I use it because it is one of the easiest to understand and communicate to other people. Also, it provides a great framework for explaining the complexities of other models.

In the DISC system,

The "D" stands for <u>dominant</u>. These people are driven to get results.

The "I" stands for <u>influencer</u>. These people are very social. They tend to be the life of the party. They never meet a stranger.

The "S" stands for <u>steady</u>. These people tend to stay calm when others panic. They are very team oriented.

The "C" stands for <u>competent</u>. These people are analytical, intuitive, and very detail oriented. The chart below gives more details about the characteristics of each.[3]

See the following chart for more detail:

C = Competence	**D = Dominant**
• Conscientious authority • Analytical • Sensitive • Factual • Diplomatic	• Driving achiever • Makes quick decisions • Takes action • Is forceful • Is time conscious
S = Steady	**I = Influencing**
• Steady worker • Loyal • Patient • Specialist • Team member	• Influential personality • Helpful • Persuasive • Emotional • Trusting

Your unique personality impacts:

- Your marriage — how you relate to your spouse.
- Your parenting — how you parent your children.
- Your work — what you do best and enjoy the most.
- How you communicate.
- How you deal with stress and the related impact on your health.
- Your approach to delegation.
- How you're motivated and try to impact the motivation of others.

I will discuss each of these to help you understand personality profiles better. My goal in this section is to give you a working knowledge of personality profiles that you can use in real time and to acquaint you with tools you can use. I am not trying to make you an expert in this material. I will begin with your personal life because it's easiest to understand. Then I will discuss organizational life.

Marriage relationship

There is an old saying that opposites attract. That isn't always true, but it was for me. The highest two areas of my profile are "D" and "C," with "S" as my third highest. If the "I" components of my personality were my heartbeat or brain waves, I would be in a coma. I have almost none. The highest areas for my wife are "I" and "S." These differences make life interesting, really fun, and at times frustrating, especially for her. We are perfect complements for each other.

We don't argue much. There are two reasons for that. Her "I" personality likes to relate and have the approval of other people. Her "S" personality likes to get along and will quickly acquiesce to what others think or want.

Parenting

Ephesians 6:3-5 tells us not to anger our children. As a practical matter, how do we keep from doing that? I was teaching a class on personality profiles once when a very agitated middle-aged man got my attention and asked if they made personality profiles for kids. I told him the profile did work for them too. As the discussion unfolded, he was actually talking about his 17-year-old son. This man was obviously a very high "D" personality. After asking a couple of questions, I discerned that his son was primarily an "S" personality. It was quite obvious to me that without some understanding and training for this man, he and his son would have trouble getting along. He would have great difficulty relating to his son in a way that would be constructive in helping him.

I heard a story about something Hallmark once did in the prison system. They offered all of the inmates free Mother's Day cards. Most of the inmates took a card and sent it to their mom. This was so well-received that they decided to do the same thing on Father's Day. To their surprise, very few of the inmates wanted a card for their father. Studies have shown a strong correlation between an absent father figure or one who doesn't relate well to his children and sons ending up in prison. It's very easy for fathers to anger their children. The more we understand about their hardwiring, the more we can relate to them in ways appropriate for each of them.

There's a difference between being fair to your kids and giving them what they need versus treating them the same. It's highly unlikely that they are the same regarding their personalities. So, how they need you to parent them will be different.

My son is very high "I" and "D." My two daughters have "S," "I," and "C" about the midline with some "D" below the midline. Trust me—they're very different in what they need. My son with the "I" and "D" personality needs a lot of freedom with some very clear boundaries to protect him. He's very capable. He's been quite successful as a business leader. But when he went to college, I knew his natural tendency would be to focus on social aspects a lot and the scholastic aspects less. I gave him a minimum GPA hurdle he had to reach each semester to stay in school. It was below his capabilities, but high enough not to cause him a problem getting a job when he graduated. I did not want to set it so high that it frustrated him and caused him to give up. But I was not willing to set it so low it would cause a problem down the road. His GPA when he graduated was within 1/10 of a percent of the target we set. I have to say, and he would agree, that he had a really great time, too.

No such target was ever established for my daughters. Why? Their natural temperaments were to try hard and be very conscientious in their studies. A target for either one of them would have simply put unnecessary stress in their lives. I was constantly telling them to do their best and not to worry, their grades would be fine. And they were. They always did better than they thought they were going to do. But the pressure of a target from me would have been hard for them even though they would have given their all to beat the target.

Work

In the work environment, people can be trained to do a great variety of things. The key is to find what they're naturally gifted at and let them refine and perfect their natural talents rather than trying to do something that takes a great deal of effort and they will never be great at. One thing you're looking for in hiring people or giving them assignments is what they are naturally good at. What do they feel they were created to do? The hardwiring, or personality profile, of an individual will give us some help in knowing what a person is naturally good at.

The "D" personality likes to initiate ideas and come up with new projects or initiatives. They like to take charge or control the project. The "I" personality likes to sell or promote the idea. They're concerned about the people aspect of the project. They like to handle the social part of the project. The "S" personality likes doing things. They enjoy doing the work. They want to do whatever it takes to make the team successful. The "C" personality likes to improve upon the idea. They are very technical and analytical. They are able to make most things work better.

The following chart illustrates the work that each personality enjoys most.

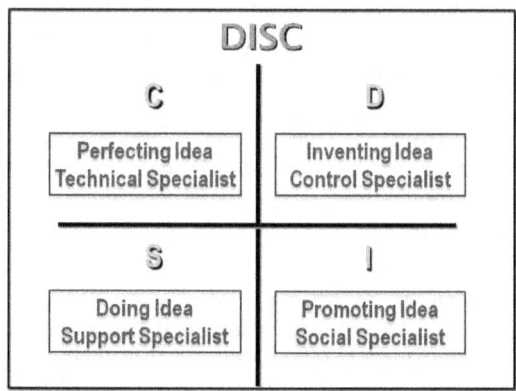

One way organizations tend to create problems in planning projects involves how people interact on the team. The "D" personality, who came up with the idea, wants to control it and does a lot of talking. "D" types tend to tell other people what to do. The "I" personality wants to be supportive. He or she starts promoting the idea and also does a lot of talking. The "S" personality, who's going to do a lot of the work, wants to be accommodating and goes along with the idea. The "C" personality tends to see flaws in the plan, but unless these types feel strongly about it they will not speak up unless called upon to point out the potential problems. They fear being ridiculed or criticized for not going along with the team. Therefore, plans are made quickly and promoted without the solid input of people who know how to execute the plan or how to improve upon it. When plans get off-track, stress is introduced into the equation and the dynamics get worse.

EXAMPLES

One time, I was touring the facility that ran a billing operation. The leader was talking about one employee who was high-energy, very likable, and talented, but who was away from their desk too much, visiting with people. I asked about the person's role. It was a data entry type function. I asked more questions and determined the individual had a primary "I" profile. I said to the leader, "This is not only non-productive for your operation but is really kind of mean to have a person with an 'I' personality in that kind of role."

I remember an employee who was promoted to another part of his organization. He had a primary "S" profile. He was steady and dependable. He did what he was told to do very well. But the leader got frustrated with him because he wanted him to take more initiative. The leader constantly made comments about his good, hard work and talked about how good he could be if he would just be proactive. What the leader did not understand was that trait didn't go with this guy's profile.

It is not uncommon for leaders to have really good employees but want and expect them to function in ways not consistent with their profiles. And, frankly, it is very easy to do this. I have done it myself a number of times. You get under pressure and need things done. You go to people who operate well in tight timeframes and don't complain about doing the extra work. But, sometimes the work itself doesn't really fit their temperament. Then, we get frustrated at the employees for not performing well at a task they're not suited for to begin with.

Sometimes, small business owners or leaders and small non-profit organizations have limited staffs and ask good people to do things they do not have the personality profile for. These individuals are quite good at certain things, but the leaders get upset at them when they don't do the work they're not suited for well.

Once, I observed a situation like this at a church where I was consulting. The church grew, and the responsibilities grew. More and more responsibilities were added to a certain person beyond his original role. This individual finally got to the point where he couldn't do it all. He could not have done some of the work well even if he had more time.

The leadership got very frustrated with this individual and now, instead of being considered one of the best in the country, he was considered incompetent.

The situation ended badly with unnecessary hurt feelings. The problem was not this individual. He was a good worker at the beginning and end of the relationship. He never really changed. The expectations changed, and the environment changed. This person was expected to do a job that no longer fit his personality profile. And now he was labeled a bad employee.

STRESS IS INTRODUCED INTO THE PROJECT

Dynamics change when stress is introduced into the equation. The chart below shows how people respond under stress.

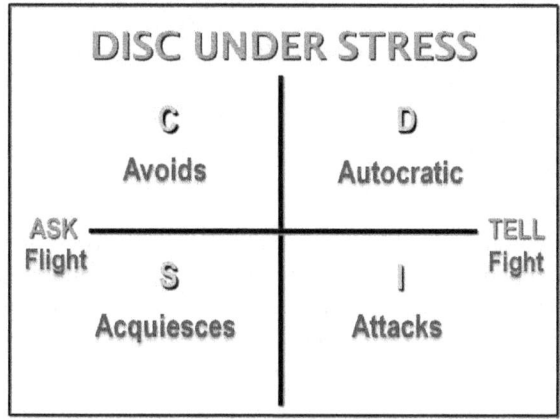

Under stress, the "D" personality becomes very autocratic. They start telling everyone what to do. The "I" personality begins to attack. This is counterintuitive. The person who has been the cheerleader and social specialist starts attacking people. This is one of the most surprising changes in behavior I see when stress is introduced. Both the "D" and "I" personalities are prepared to fight when stressed.

The "S" personality wants to make peace. They will give up their position to make others happy. Their stance is, "I'll do whatever you want me to do. Can't we just all get along?" The "C" personality tends to be quiet and reflective. Unless they feel strongly about it, they may not speak up unless called upon. Also, they will get very upset if they feel any criticism for the failure is being directed toward them.

These dynamics illustrate how organizational life can become messy. Stress is usually introduced when something has gone wrong. The personalities doing the talking, the "D" and "I," don't know how to do the work or improve on the work but are giving the directions. The personalities with the most insight in how to get the project back on track, the "S" and "C," are acquiescing or avoiding the discussion altogether.

In this situation, a good leader needs to recognize the personality profile of each team member and the strengths each brings to the table. The leader needs to draw the "S" and "C" personalities into the discussion to get their expert perspective. Then, the "D" personality needs to chart a course, and the "I" personality needs to sell the new approach.

HCA went through a major merger in the 1990s. For my department, the teams of three former companies were being merged. I volunteered to handle the planning process to integrate the three former departments into one. All four major personality types were represented on the leadership teams of the three different departments. As you would expect, the person in the room with the highest "D" personality, besides myself, wanted to talk first and often. Next to speak were the ones that had the highest "I" components. As the facilitator, I let them talk. After an appropriate time, I asked that we listen to other team members. I called on the "S" personalities first. They knew most about how to get the work done. Next, I called on the "C" personalities. They tended to be most shy and generally would not talk unless asked their opinion in group settings. Yet, they will identify potential problems that no one else saw, ask deeper questions, and improve upon a good idea.

After hearing from the "S" and "C" personalities, I asked the "D" personalities for their perspective on executing and controlling the project. I asked the "I" for input on how this would impact people and be received by them.

When we combined all these perspectives, we had a much better plan which engaged the entire team with their unique perspectives. It worked with fewer problems and adjustments later than if we had used a different approach.

Communicating

Our personality profile impacts how we like to receive communication. The "D" personality wants to know "the bottom line." They are focused on the action they will take as a result of the communication. The "I" personality wants communication to be fun and interesting. They want to know about the impact on people. The "S" personality wants the communication to be structured and non-confrontational. They do not want to feel like they need to make dramatic changes. This reminds me of former President George Bush Sr. who would often say, "Let's stay the course." The "C" personality wants communication to be factual. They remind me of the old TV show, *Dragnet*, and Officer Joe Friday, whose favorite line was, "Just the facts, ma'am."

Here's an important thing to remember about personality profiles and communication. Our profile determines how we like to receive communication and thus how we tend to communicate with other people. For example, with my "D" and "C" personality, I like to hear the bottom line first. Then, depending on my level of interest, I may drill into very significant detail.

> **"What we have here is a failure to communicate."[4]**

The question we have to ask ourselves in organizational life is, "How do the people we're dealing with like to receive communication?" Unless we're dealing with people with our same profile, the answer will be that they like to receive communication in a different way than we like to give it. As a practical matter, this means we need to understand other people's profiles and structure our communication approach according to their needs, not ours.

I get frustrated when people try to give me a lot of detail before I understand the big picture and the bottom line. This is why, in corporate presentations, you have an Executive Summary followed by detail. In most important business meetings, you have "D" personality profiles at the table that are going to make a decision pretty quickly, and you have to get your point across before you lose their attention. You also have "S" and "C" personalities in the room that want more information. The "D" personality is often going to ask their perspective before implementing a final decision. So you have to have the structure detail for them. If you don't have it, they will bring up all kinds of questions that have to be answered before the final decision is made.

WHAT YOU WILL BE RESPECTED FOR

When dealing with people, it's important to know what they will respect you for during the interaction. The "D" personality respects you for speed. They want you to get to the bottom line so they can make a decision and move on. They don't like to chitchat.

By contrast, the "I" personality very much enjoys chitchat. You need to slow down, take time, and use great verbal care and concern to maintain the relationship with them.

You don't want to be in a hurry with an "S" type personality either. They like harmony and a sense of friendship. They also know how things work, so you need to show your competence with them. You can't gloss over things and maintain their respect. The "C" personality takes that a step further. You need to have precise standards for what you expect. These folks respect authoritative standards, not your personal opinion, unless they consider you an expert.

FEARS

You will be more effective in dealing with people if you keep their fears in mind. The "D" personality is very competitive. Therefore, they fear losing. If at all possible, never set up a situation where they personally perceive you are in competition with them. Either defer to them or create a win-win situation. In win-lose situations, it will be a bitter fight to the end. Also, the "D" personality does not like scrutiny. They like big challenges and freedom to do things their way. If you make them feel like you're looking over their shoulder, you will meet a great deal of resistance.

The "I" hates loss of approval. These folks can accept constructive criticism. The key is to make sure they understand you still like them and still care about them. If they sense they have lost your approval, they tend to go on the attack. Also, they don't like a fixed environment. They are free spirits and like the freedom not to be tied down. They don't like budgets either. I know; I'm married to an "I" personality. The review of the household budget is like spousal abuse to them. If there had been a "1-800 budget abuse hotline," it would have gotten calls from my house over the years. "I" personality types just don't like limits. Also, they don't like their time audited. If you have a significant other in your life with an "I" personality and they agree to do three things in a day, when they tell you they got two done, brag on them. They expect to be acknowledged for the two things they did. If you focus on the one thing that didn't get done and try to show them where they could've been more efficient with their time, you're only going to hurt their feelings and eventually make them mad.

The "S" personality is easy-going, and they don't like big or sudden changes. These represent a loss of security for them, which is very important. They like tradition and sameness. They have a sense of how things should work and a strong dislike for unethical procedure, and they will resist it.

The "C" personality hates criticism. It's extremely difficult to find a way to offer constructive criticism to the "C" personality so that they don't take offense. They are perfectionist oriented. Therefore, they hate making mistakes. They're very hard on themselves and others. In the spiritual world, we would say they tend to be legalists. Also, they hate incompetent supervisors. The challenging thing is who they consider incompetent. Often, that is most other personality profiles. The "C" personalities consider themselves to be the experts unless they are dealing with another "C" personality of recognized "guru status." I know! I led the audit department of HCA for many years with a primary "D," secondary "C," and tertiary "S" personality profile. This profile equipped me to lead the department. But I'm sure there were many folks over the years who thought I wasn't as smart as they were when it came to the technical details. And the truth is they were right.

Response to policy manuals

The "D" personality is not interested in the policy manual. They're okay with one existing as long as you don't try to apply it to them. They don't like to be controlled by policies and procedures, but they're fine with using the manual to control others.

The "I" type can't find their manual and has a strong distaste for policies and procedures.

The "S" personality always follows the manual. They understand the process and respect it. They wrote the initial policy manual and will likely do the revisions.

The "C" personality has great respect for the policy manual, particularly if it has clear standards that make sense to them. They don't often have to look things up in the manual because they know exactly what it says. As a "D" personality, I seldom looked things up in the policy manual. However, a "C" personality was in the office next to me. I would simply shout next-door and ask him what the manual said. He could always quote it for me.

Your Style Impacts the Team You Need

I'm sure many people have the mistaken impression that you must have a "D" personality profile to lead. That's not true. We see leaders with different profiles. What is true is that your style determines how you're going to tend to approach leadership and, therefore, the profiles you need around you to complement what you're trying to accomplish.

Delegation

Personality profiles affect how and to whom we should delegate certain projects. The "D" personality wants general direction and a lot of freedom. They like to do new things. They get bored with the status quo very easily. My son, Scott, is like this. He is an "I" and "D" personality. He likes a lot of freedom and broad boundaries. He lived on St. John Island as leader of an ecotourism resort. The freedom he was given in that job fit his style very well.

The "I" personality likes projects dealing with people. They don't want a lot of detail work. They prefer frequent conversation with their manager. They also like freedom and don't care for details. My wife, Debbie, is like this. She likes a great deal of freedom and doesn't like to get bogged down with detail. But she does like to get actively engaged.

The "S" personality likes clear guidelines and the ability to work with the team. They want an environment that is not competitive and free from conflict. My eldest daughter, Allyson, is like this. In college, she was majoring in fashion merchandising, which fit the skills and passions she had. However, as she got into the program, she realized the culture of the work environment was highly competitive rather than team oriented and the best jobs were in major cities where she did not think she wanted to spend her life. She assessed other career paths that would use her natural talents in a more team-oriented culture. Today, she has a job that matches her personality.

One word of caution is due. "S" personalities are doers. They get things done and their managers like to keep them happy. Sometimes, because they do things so well, they get promoted to positions that don't match their "S" personality.

The reason the Peter Principle exists—the tendency to promote people to their level of incompetence—is that "S" personalities often get promoted to stressful leadership roles they ultimately don't like.

The "C" personality likes analytical projects. They need a clear standard to meet and like detailed explanations about the project. My younger daughter, Kelsey, has a lot of "C" personality along with good components of "S" and "I" like her older sister. She likes clear standards of what is expected. She will even ask for permission to change channels on the TV or turn it off if she's not alone in the room.

Motivation

The "D" personality is very competitive and is motivated by accomplishments. I'm like that. I like to do things that people say can't be done or have never been done.

The "I" personality likes to be seen. They are motivated by recognition. My son is like this. He took great pride in driving a thirty-year-old orange International Scout in high school. There wasn't another one like it around, and it drew attention to him.

The "S" personality is motivated to get the job done and done well, with others. They are motivated to maintain harmony. Often, they are the peacemakers on the team. My daughter Allyson is like this in the workplace. Kelsey is often like this at home or school.

The "C" personality is motivated to improve things. They hate criticism and are motivated to do things with perfection. Where the "D" and "I" personalities both love public attention and praise, the "C" personality is shy and appreciates individual, private praise.

People would be easier to understand if they simply fit only one of these four categories. But it doesn't work that way. People are a blend of all four styles. This can get complicated very quickly. Using a good profiling system like DISC gives you a good written and graphic perspective of an individual's personality.

If you do not use personality profiles correctly, you may have good people who are headaches because they don't fit their roles or because of how you deal with them.

YOUR PERSONALITY PROFILE DOES NOT EXCUSE YOUR BAD BEHAVIOR

I have a word of caution for those individuals who would read this section of the book and say, "Well this is how I'm made. That's how I naturally respond, so everybody around me just needs to get used to it." I have this to say to you. There is a reason why God did not hardwire your mind to your mouth. One is practical and one is spiritual. In other words, you don't have to say everything you think. I remember many times when my dad and I were working around the barn or in the field together and he would speak his mind about what was going on in the family, church, or community. One thing he often said to me before we left the field was, "Boy, you know you don't have to go back to the house and tell everything you know."

I said all that to say this: You don't have to act in accordance with how you think. You can't say, "I'm just hardwired to think and act this way," because that ignores the fact that man is the height of God's creation. Unlike animals that act only on instinct, you're given the power of choice. You get to choose your action or reaction to any event or stimulus. I would add that for those born of the Spirit of God, this is even more so the case. For the believer, the Spirit of God lives within us to convict us of wrong and guide us in doing what is pure and right. Even then we have a choice. We learn in God's word that the mind guided by the Spirit is life and the mind guided by the flesh, our natural instinct, is death (Romans 8:6). I read a great book many years ago by Tim LaHaye called *The Spirit Controlled Temperament*. The point of the book is that no matter what our natural hardwiring is, there are strengths in the Spirit of God for every weakness we have. We have the choice to be guided by our natural instincts or to be guided by and act on the leadership of God's Spirit in our life. Therefore, we have no excuse for any of our instinctual bad behavior.

Other profile systems

I have used some form of DISC profile for understanding my team for many years. There are a number of other good profiling systems on the market. I discovered one by Axiometrics International (A*i*) which I use in concert with

DISC. As an analogy, if DISC is an x-ray of your personality, A*i* is an MRI of your personality. It goes much deeper, and it is difficult to manipulate compared to simpler profiles.

For all leadership/management positions, I use the A*i* "Professional Profile" and "Professional Competencies (120) Profile." These show people's top ten leadership strengths and their top five areas for development. They also give views into leadership competencies as per the charts below.

Professional Profile – For leaders/managers

- Ten top competencies
- Five key development areas
- Leadership/management competencies
- Will you fit into the organization?
- How well can you manage yourself?
- How well can you think, solve problems, and make decisions?
- Can you lead?

Professional Competencies (120) assessment

Assessment of strengths/weaknesses in ten key areas of leadership:

- Interpersonal relationships
- Problem solving
- Decision making
- Time management
- Leadership
- Training and development
- Coaching and counseling
- Administrative
- Account development and management
- Management and supervision

To access the A*i* profiles, go to https://www.axiometrics.org. Once you are at the website, the login code is LEADERSHIP. You are invited to complete the profile and receive the "Career Pathfinder" report for free. The Axiometrics

PEOPLE

reports referenced above and their prices are listed on the website. You may purchase these at a 10% discount. (Note: these items will not work on mobile devices.)

To access a DISC profile, go to www.48days.com and find personality profiles. When you're at the shopping cart, type the word "Leon" in the coupon box and you will get a 10% discount on this profile.

Chapter 12

CHOOSE THE RIGHT TEAM

> **Thought:**
> How much more fun would leadership be if you had confidence in choosing your team well?

"So now send me a man skilled to work in gold, silver, bronze and iron."

2 Chronicles 2:7 (ESV)

One of the most important decisions Jesus ever made was choosing His disciples. After all, He knew that His ministry on earth would be relatively short, only three years. He knew that He was to train and empower twelve disciples to carry on His work and that He would impact all of human history through them. In fact, just before His death He told them that they would do more than He had done.

> *"Never doubt that a small group of thoughtful, committed people can change the world. Indeed, it is the only thing that ever has."* [5]

One man told his son, "Hire people who are mission driven—people who share your vision. If you don't, your business will struggle, or may never get off the ground. One of the reasons Steve Jobs is the entrepreneur of the era is because he has missionaries inside his company as well as outside."[6]

WHAT A DIFFERENCE ONE PERSON CAN MAKE

Some people believe it's hard for one person to make a difference. Others have seen what a difference one person can make. When it comes to leadership roles, I have always been amazed at the difference one person can make. In my experience with HCA Physician Services, I had one division within the company where the leadership was not strong. Out of 12 divisions in the entire company, I got more complaints out of this division than the other 11 combined. I went through the process of making the leadership change and put Louis in place in that division. Within 18 months, I got more unsolicited compliments out of that division than all the other 11 combined. The difference that made in my life as a leader and for my organization was so significant it's hard to describe.

Suffice it to say that one person can make an incredible difference. If an employee doesn't fit the organization for any reason, it is extremely painful. When you replace them with someone who is really good in the position, the difference is staggering.

God gave people natural gifts and talents that are to be exercised for the good of mankind while we're on this earth. He also gave spiritual gifts to be used for building up the church. These are outlined in Ephesians 4:11-12. The world works much better when people are working within the talent and gift set that God gave them. When they get out of place, you have a problem. Pride and greed often drive people to want more power or more material things. Many people are lured from their strengths to get more power or money and begin to

Chapter 12 – Choose the Right Team

operate outside their gifting. It's quite common in the non-profit and ministry world for founding leaders to want to be something they are not in order to maintain power and control. They may stray so far outside of their gift set that they lose effectiveness or eventually fail altogether.

It should be no surprise that one of the most important jobs of the leader is picking the right people who fit their roles and can be successful within the culture and environment in which they operate. People who are not good at choosing a team can't be successful in the long run. They will be miserable, and so will the people on their team. Further, these leaders will have ongoing difficulties with delegation. If they cannot choose well who to bring on the team, they cannot choose well in delegating work to others.

THE RIGHT PUZZLE PIECE

Jim Collins in *Good to Great* uses the analogy of putting the right person in the right seat on the bus.[7] That's a good analogy. But I like the analogy of the right puzzle piece, given the growing complexity of organizations with multiple business units, departments, and functions, often coupled with heavily-matrixed organization structures. It is one thing to find people that can do the job. It's quite another to find people that can do the job within a given culture and with the team they need to work with. To me, that's what makes selection more like completing a puzzle than the simple view of right person, right seat.

It's a real problem when people don't fit the puzzle. That's one reason why this whole leadership thing is so much more complicated when you actually have to do it than it sounds and appears to people who have never done it.

Choosing Teams on the Playground

We played ball at recess when I was a kid in grade school. Two people always identified themselves as leaders and chose teams. One would choose a player, and then the other would choose. This continued until everyone was chosen. The best players were chosen first and the weakest players last. You always knew how good people thought you were based on how soon you were chosen. The process actually worked quite well in choosing talent. The leaders had observed you playing and knew what you were capable of. They assigned positions on the field based on their observation of people's aptitude for those positions.

Though this entire process was informal, the kids who were leaders did a good job of identifying talent and putting people in the right position so that the teams were fairly evenly matched.

Choosing the Team in an Organization

We finish school, go to college, get a job, and then get frustrated with this process of choosing people. It seemed so simple when we were in grade school. Why is that? We had multiple chances to observe the talent of the individuals over time before we chose them to be on our team.

We should not overlook the value of prayer as we choose our teams. Jesus had great insights into people, but He still relied on prayer as He chose the twelve disciples. Also, Jesus chose a number of different personality profiles as His disciples because He knew that was what was required to get the job done.

When we hire people outside the organization, they come to an interview with a résumé and a game face. We have not had the opportunity to observe them nor do we know which position they play best. At the end of the interview, what we really know is how they come across in an interview. Plus, individuals and companies are making a living teaching people how to prepare for and handle interviews to get the job they want. Candidates are coming to the interview with great preparation. They are better at controlling the interview process than many executives who conduct the interviews.[8]

Next, let's look at what a good recruiting process looks like. We will also evaluate the common mistakes made in the recruiting and interview processes.

COMMON MISTAKES IN RECRUITING

There are many mistakes you can make in the recruiting process. I know! I've made all of them. But if you do a poor job on any one of these, the process breaks down, yielding a poor result.

Mistake #1 – Not looking at the whole person

Looking at the whole person includes the individual's life before the things you see on the résumé and those that go beyond the résumé.

Preparation
- Education
- Experience
- Accomplishments

Pre-Résumé
- Calling
- Passion
- Personality
- Experiences

Post-Résumé
- Expectations
- Potential
- Attitude

After giving it much thought, the visual above is what I would use to evaluate the whole person in an interview. Some of this I learned from my first boss. Some of it I learned by experience over many years. And, frankly, some of it I realize I should have done after studying Scripture and reflecting on the matter.

One of the deficiencies I see in most interview processes is that much of the process is based on looking at people's preparation, i.e. their experience and accomplishments.

My first boss spent the first part of the interview asking about the candidate's childhood, siblings, and parents. I used to think this quite odd. I thought an interview started with the résumé—not before it. Then, I realized he was finding out a great deal about some very major influences on that person's life that shaped who that person was. He understood that what parents did and the associated work ethic would have a great influence on the candidate. He also understood that siblings have a great deal to do with how a person interacts as a member of a team. He understood that difficulties, challenges, and successes from early childhood would greatly impact the candidate's performance as an adult.

A pastor I know says that one of the most significant influences preparing him for his role in the church was the work he did for his dad, who owned a TV store. He says that his interaction with the public did more to prepare him for his role as pastor than some of the things he learned in seminary.

I wish now that I had focused even more time on candidates' personal lives before their work experience began. I wish I had asked more questions that would have helped me understand their calling in life and passion. Often, people are driven by something that's happened to them in life having nothing to do with what is on their résumé. Earlier I mentioned a quality officer at a major hospital I know who has a passion for quality even beyond the norm for that role. The reason is that she lost a teenage son to a clinical error in a hospital. I assure you she approaches her role with much more passion and zeal than what is typical.

People's personalities are developed long before they enter the workforce. Understanding their unique personalities as I discussed previously is key to knowing if they will fit certain roles. One thing I insisted on was having insights into a candidate's personality before they came in for the interview.

People's work experiences and accomplishments can be gleaned from the résumé. But I learned by experience that it's wise to go beyond their accomplishments and experience to thinking about the future. I learned that it was important to ask about expectations for the future and try to assess their potential for growth with the organization.

I also learned that it is best to ask open-ended questions rather than leading questions in the interview process. I learned and developed this approach from my internal audit experience. It made a huge difference in the quality of my interviews. With open ended questions, people have no idea what answer will sound the best to you. Their best option is simply to answer completely and honestly. I tried to ask "most" and "least" questions; for example, "What did you like most about this situation or these people and what did you like least?" This way the candidate cannot anticipate what you want the answer to be. They simply must answer candidly.

Mistake # 2 – Not spending time and money on personality profiles

Without a clear understanding of the DISC personality profile needed, anybody with related experience is a potential candidate. You could potentially do in-depth interviews of a lot of people you shouldn't spend time with. You may hire the one you like best rather than the one best suited for the job.

In business, church, and ministry organizations, I have dealt with this issue many times. A person comes highly recommended for the job. The leaders/managers feel like they just have to have this individual. Before I would interview them, I would establish the ideal profile and the acceptable range of personality profiles for this particular job. I would also make some other inquiries into why a certain profile was needed to do a particular job.

Next, I would require that a profile be done for each candidate before beginning the interview process. There were many times when the profile of the person the leaders thought they had to have was well outside the range they defined as ideal or acceptable. Sometimes they hired the individual anyway because they liked the person and thought they could make it work. I never saw it work long-term, and usually it was a disaster.

I'll admit I did something similar myself. I knew the best profile for a particular position in our billing office was a "D" and "C." We had a person in an accounting role with a "D" and "I" profile. We reasoned that because he had the accounting degree and experience he could adapt to the job. I liked him a lot, and he was a really hard worker. I was wrong! It didn't work out.

Some leaders and managers are not willing to spend the money on personality profiles for key candidates. There is an expression that fits this. It's called being "penny wise and pound foolish." I personally saved many hours and thousands of dollars on travel by not interviewing people who had enticing résumés but personality profiles that didn't fit the job. I also saved the company many more thousands of dollars by not putting the wrong person in a position and having poor performance or the enormous cost of making a change later. On top of that is the cost of having the wrong person in place for a period of time.

I'm familiar with a national ministry that recently made a change with one city director. The person clearly did not fit the role. The ministry could have spent $300 for a personality profile, known this on the front end, and avoided making that hiring decision. Instead, they spent $300,000 over two years for very little results and had to start over trying to find the right person for the role.

Using personality profiles does take some time and money. The problems they avoid and the "opportunity costs" they avoid usually have a payoff of at least tenfold.

Mistake # 3 – Not understanding the person's calling in life

People can learn to do many things. But all people have a special calling in life—a purpose that God created them for (Psalm 139:16). Taking the time to find that out is key. If they can accomplish their calling while contributing directly in the role you are interviewing them for, you are making a potential long-term hire. To determine their calling, find out what they're passionate about. Ask them what they've always been good at. Find out what gives them joy and raises their energy versus what frustrates them and tires them out.

Ask people what they have always done well—things people seem to always want them to do—and brag on them when they do those things.[9] Ask people, "Is there something you enjoy doing so much and do so well that you feel like you were just made to do it?" Ask them, "Is there something you enjoy doing so much and that makes you feel so good that you would still do it if you didn't get paid for it?"

Mistake # 4 – Letting the candidates find you rather than seeking out the ones most suited for the job

It's much easier to run an ad and let people looking for a job find you. For key positions, it is worth the time and effort to determine who is best in the field

Chapter 12 – Choose the Right Team

and to see if they match the values and vision of your organization. One of the best people I've ever hired was not looking for a job at the time I hired her. In fact, it took three different phone calls for me to get her to even agree to an interview. Often, the people best for the job aren't looking for a job. You have to go find them.

Mistake # 5 – Focusing only on your goals and not on the candidate's goals

Some leaders, in fact most, leave out one very important dynamic in the interview process. They are pursuing what they want, trying to fill their needs and determining if the person they're interviewing can do the job and is willing to take it. Something critically important is to determine if this person truly wants the job. Not from the standpoint of "I must work and pay the bills," but from the standpoint of "Is this consistent with my personal goals and do I really want this job?" Does this job fit the vision, passion, calling, and goals of the candidate? As I mentioned earlier, one of the best hires I was ever fortunate enough to make was a person who didn't think she even wanted to interview for the job. Let me tell you about Claudia.

Claudia may have had more educational credentials than anybody I ever recruited. She was highly personable, articulate, and professional. She knew what she was about more than anyone I had ever met. She worked at a firm that worked for HCA and was quite happy there. I talked to her on the phone three different times about coming to an interview. She nicely declined each time. She did not want to send mixed signals to her firm, and she really wasn't interested in making a change.

This intrigued me. I asked her why she was so content at the firm. She was able to clearly and passionately articulate her career goals and the impact she wanted to have. She clearly fit the "cathedral builder" analogy. I listened intently to her goals. Then there was this magic moment where I got very excited and passionate. I told her that I understood her commitment to her firm. I also told her that I thought she would be very happy there. However, I told her that I thought she could be even happier in the job I was recruiting her for. I went on for quite some time explaining how her passions, dreams, and life goals could be carried out at HCA even better than at her firm.

That began a process. I spoke to her three times in person and finally was able to recruit her into HCA. In her specialty, she became like the E. F. Hutton in the company. After a few months, when Claudia spoke, everyone listened. She made enormous contributions to the company. Every time I spoke to her in subsequent years, she still loved her role.

Claudia was one of the best hires I ever made. But the face-to-face interview process would never have started with me focused on my goals or what was good for the company. I had to understand her goals and explain to her clearly how the company could help her meet them before I could hire her.

I continued to find that recruiting the very best people requires this approach. Often, the best people are not knocking on your door asking you to hire them. They are content working somewhere else where they are admired, respected, have great influence, and are paid and treated well. To get them, you have to show them how they can achieve more of their own goals in your job and your company than where they are. Currently, this requires that you listen intently to them about their goals and what they like about where they work. This is very counterintuitive to most leaders.

Mistake # 6 – Pride – Insisting on the right of first refusal

Often, the hiring leaders/managers talk about the job and the company too early in the process. They want to convince the individual that he or she should want to work for the company and why they should want this particular job. The problem with that is you don't know yet if you want the individual in the company or the job.

To my chagrin, as a young hiring manager I did this once. The candidate was thrilled about the company, excited about the job, and asked when he could start. I sat there dumbfounded, realizing I hadn't even interviewed him yet and didn't know if I even wanted him!

Two of the reasons so many people get placed in the wrong jobs are poor interviewing techniques and human nature. Human nature is for candidates to come in and sell themselves as being a great fit for the job. Why? Our ego causes us to want to have the "right of refusal." If the candidates cannot sell themselves and get the offer, they have no "right of refusal" and they may feel rejected.

Conversely, the hiring leaders/managers often feel the same way. If they have a strong viable candidate on paper, they want to make sure the candidate is impressed enough that they can hire the candidate if they want to. Therefore, if you're not careful, you have two individuals telling each other what they think the other wants to hear without doing the hard work of determining if they really fit the job.

Mistake # 7 – Letting the candidate take charge

The next mistake is letting the candidate lead the interview. I've had many try this, especially those with "D" personality profiles. They talk about themselves and try to sell you on why they fit the job. Generally, if allowed, they will ask you a lot of questions about the job. If you answer them, it's human nature for them to position their comments and answers to your subsequent questions to fit what they think you're looking for. The value of the hiring professional taking the lead and asking structured, open-ended questions is that this scenario is completely avoided. They don't know what you're looking for and can only answer candidly. If they are not answering candidly, they will come across as shallow or contradictory. I learned these questioning approaches through my audit experience.

UNDERSTAND THEIR RÉSUMÉ

Ask the individuals what they liked most and least about each of the jobs on their résumé. From this, I got a sense of the types of tasks, activities, and environments they like most, as well as those that de-motivate them. I've had times where, from a practical standpoint, the interview was over after these questions because I could see so many similarities between what they didn't like and what would be required in the job for which they were interviewing. I would continue to be kind but also honest with the candidate. Then, I would give them the chance to ask questions or talk about themselves so that they would not feel badly about the interview, but would also be respectful of their time and mine.

It is common for leaders to determine that individuals are only interested in the job they're interviewing for. I found it especially useful to probe deeply about what they liked and disliked about their last job. Were they outgrowing their job? Were they feeling restrained in their last job and looking for new opportunities? Were they looking for a slower, steadier pace with less change and therefore less opportunity? Probing deeply in these areas will give you a much better perspective on whether these individuals "fit your puzzle."

Personal Background

Try to understand individuals' personal backgrounds better. Ask what they like most and least about themselves. This information will give you a good idea of their self-awareness, self-esteem, and ego. People who like a lot of things about themselves and can't think of anything they like least are usually going to be harder to lead. Generally, they have high ego needs, don't work well with teams, and don't take direction well. That doesn't mean you shouldn't hire them. Certain personality profiles are that way, and there are positions they fit. But be aware of what you are getting.

By contrast, individuals too hard on themselves may have poor self-esteem. These people often are overly critical and negative. They can be generally critical of their teammates, their supervisors, and the organization.

You're really looking for a healthy balance—people who are aware of their strengths but also their weaknesses and can keep the two in perspective. It's good to ask about personal and professional goals they've achieved in the past that gave them the most satisfaction. Also, ask about their biggest disappointments or failures, both personal and professional. I personally like people who have had some failures in life and were able to learn from them and put them in perspective. Since I have their personality profiles, I already know a lot about their personal traits. Sometimes, I ask follow-up questions.

Their personality is only part of the picture, though. I want to find out about life experiences that have shaped how they think and feel. I want to know what they are passionate about. I want to see if they have a sense of "calling," i.e., "this is what I was made to do—this is my unique purpose in life."

Attitude

Our thoughts and attitudes are very important to God. Scripture is clear that God looks at people's hearts before selecting them for significant roles in His kingdom. For example, God looked at the heart and selected David to be king over Israel even though his brothers were bigger, stronger, and looked the part. Samuel was surprised by God's choice because he was, in effect, looking at the résumés. All of David's brothers seemed more qualified than David. After all, he was only a young shepherd.

Chapter 12 – Choose the Right Team

"For as he thinketh in his heart, so is he."
Proverbs 23:7 (KJV)

When we are held accountable by God, He will not look at just what we did, but He will also look at our motives and attitudes. Wise and godly leaders will similarly discern the attitudes of people they hire and give significant job assignments to.

Ask candidates what they like most and least about peers, subordinates, and past leaders. Take your time. These discussions will give you great insights about candidates' attitudes toward other people. If your leadership style is more like one of their favorite leaders from the past, you have a better chance of a good relationship. If your style is closer to the leaders they liked least, the relationship may not work. The same is true for their peer group.

If the individuals you're hiring will supervise others, you want to understand their attitude toward subordinates. If their view is not consistent with the culture you are trying to create for your organization, you should not put them into the position. Also, ask them what their leaders, peers, and subordinates like most and least about them. This will give you a sense of their self-awareness.

I remember Frank, who was hired by someone else but eventually reported to me. Over time, I noticed that he was very critical of every person he'd ever worked for. In his mind, they were all "idiots" or "jerks." It didn't take me long to figure out that no matter what I did, that would be his final assessment of me. Sure enough, after he left my department and went to another part of the company, he began "badmouthing" me. If I had been the original hiring professional using this interviewing approach, that characteristic would have been identified during the interview, and he would not have been brought into the company.

If individuals have never liked any organization they've worked for, there is very little chance they will like your organization. I never experienced an exception to that rule. To the contrary, Frank and many others like him convinced me how reliable it is. Ask what they like most and least about the organization or company they just left or are considering leaving. Listen for aspects of the culture they liked or didn't like. Listen for policies and procedures that annoyed them. Compare these to your own organization to see if they would be any happier. Listen for a critical attitude toward the organization. If you happen to know it's a good organization and they are very critical, it could be a red flag for you. If you happen to know it's not a good organization, listen and see if they can tactfully explain what they didn't like without a critical spirit. Remember that the attitudes they have toward their former organization will come with them to your organization.

FUTURE EXPECTATIONS AND POTENTIAL

Ask questions about their compensation history. Ask what they liked most and least about their overall compensation package. This will give you an idea of what they value in a package. Some people like their salary packages with limited equity or bonus potential. Some people prefer less base play with more significant bonus or equity opportunities. Knowing this will help you structure a package that fits them best if you want to hire them.

The compensation discussion will give you an understanding of what they have become accustomed to in the past and their expectations about the future. If they have become accustomed to healthy annual increases and you're hiring them at the top end of your pay range, you already know those kinds of increases will not be possible in your organization going forward. Having a clear understanding of that will keep you from making mistakes.

Ask questions about their future aspirations and goals. Ask about their mobility. These things may give you some insights into their potential and desire to grow with your organization.

Talk more about what they think, and avoid questions they can easily answer with what they believe you want to hear. I found that an interview following this simple approach, along with a personality profile done in advance, is superior to most other approaches.

If you are not good at choosing the *right* people for your team, then many will seem like headaches to you, not assets.

Chapter 13

MAKE SURE PEOPLE STILL FIT THEIR JOBS

> **Thought:**
> How effective could my organization be if everybody on the team played their role well and were highly motivated? How much potential and productivity is my organization losing because I have people who do not fit?

"You shall speak to all the skillful persons whom I have endowed with the spirit of wisdom, that they make Aaron's garments..."

Exodus 28:3

Sometimes leaders come to the realization, "Oh, my gosh! I have people in place who don't fit the job. I have a 'square peg in a round hole.'" Put another way, "My people aren't the puzzle pieces I need anymore. They are either too small, too large, or just the wrong shape for what I need."

 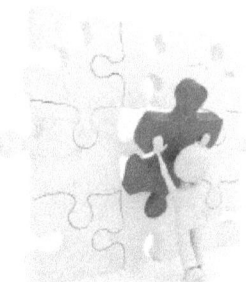

It's not uncommon for leaders to be frustrated because a number of their people don't seem to be meeting their expectations. The natural assumption of some leaders is, "I have bad people. I need to 'fire' them and get some different people." This is a simplistic and often counterproductive way to look at and deal with the situation. Start by understanding the reasons for underperformance.[10]

- Did they used to fit, but the circumstances or work environment changed?
- Has there been a change in the people they work with and around?
- Has something changed in another area of their life that is impacting their performance? Is this change temporary or permanent?
- Were they ever suited for this position, or was it just a bad hire?
- Has their performance actually changed, or is it my attitude toward them that has changed? Am I under a lot of stress, causing me to be more critical of the team?

The answers to these questions give some idea as to the path you should take. Let's explore further by asking the question, "Can the needed results be achieved with this person in the job?" If the answer is no, the only fair thing to do is make a change. But many leaders seem very reluctant to do this. Some don't do it at all. And many do it much later than they should. In fact, many wait until they are in crisis mode and mad or upset before they take any action. This only makes the situation worse or causes them to handle it poorly—which in turn makes them more reluctant to make a timely change the next time they need to.

TAKE A BIBLICAL VIEW

God created everyone with the ability to do something well and enjoy it. Why are leaders so reluctant to make a change? If people go to a neurologist because a tumor is putting pressure on the brain and giving them severe headaches, does the neurologist feel badly about suggesting brain surgery? Does the neurologist apologize for suggesting brain surgery? Does the neurologist dread doing the surgery? Obviously, you want a brain surgeon who is empathetic. But do you really want a brain surgeon who dreads doing surgery? I don't.

So what about people in a job that doesn't fit? Don't you think they feel some pressure? Don't you think they feel uncomfortable and perhaps even miserable? So if you move down the path of relieving the pressure, are you hurting these people or helping them? Our hesitancy is based upon a wrong view of this entire situation.

> *"But speaking the truth in love, we are to grow up in all aspects into Him..."*
>
> *Ephesians 4:15*

A major reason we aren't willing to make personnel changes is that we view these people through a paradigm we learned in organizations rather than from the Bible.

Let's take a practical example. I observed a lot of hospital CEOs over many years. Some didn't appear great to me, but they had the good fortune of being in growth markets, and had stellar facilities, excellent medical staffs, great leadership teams, and good labor markets. They did not build or select the teams; they were just fortunate enough to be placed there. They were given the invisible "hero" label.

Conversely, I saw some CEOs that were exceptionally smart, worked really hard, and had stellar values. They had the challenge of being in difficult markets, needing access to additional capital, and having challenging medical staffs, weaker leadership teams, and an overall tougher labor market. These CEOs seldom got the "hero" label no matter how hard they worked to improve their situations.

These experiences convinced me I should throw away the invisible "hero" and "goat" labels. When I did, my whole view changed of removing people who didn't fit the puzzle.

Are individuals in difficult situations bad people or poor employees? Maybe it's not their fault. If they never really fit the role, it's the leader's fault for putting them into it. If a team member is undermining them, it's the team member's fault. If the culture is a barrier for them, that's the problem.

No matter how good we become at selecting people, most of us are going to make a mistake. The question is: What are we going to do about it? Unless it's really bad or until it gets really bad, most leaders do nothing. After all, it's a messy job. In the traditional view, we tell ourselves we have to "fire" the person. We hate that. And I hope we do hate it anytime it's framed that way. We feel bad for the person and about ourselves for the perceived "negative" action we're getting ready to take.

Using a more biblical view, we are not always saying someone in such a situation is a bad person or a bad employee. I generally don't like to use the term "fire" or "terminate."

COMPASSION

So here's the question—are we being kind to people when we leave them where they don't fit? Are we helping them when we leave them in a situation where they can't do the job well? The simple answer is—no. In fact, it is just plain insensitive and maybe mean.[11]

The most compassionate thing we can do for these people is to help them find a puzzle they fit. Please notice, I said *help*. They have to work with us and own the responsibility for accomplishing the transition. They are more likely to cooperate wholeheartedly if we kindly, clearly, and compassionately explain to them it's better for them, better for the team, and better for the organization.

I have a good friend named Jim Patton. Jim got a degree from a technical school with the goal of becoming an HVAC repairman making $20 an hour. He thought this would provide a good living and all he wanted out of life at the time. He tells the story in his excellent book, *Life in the Turn Lane*, of how his boss put his arm around him one day and said, "You're just not very good at this." He let Jim go. Jim was devastated and I'm sure his boss felt bad. But it was the best thing that could have happened for Jim. His boss did him a favor. Jim was made to be a "dealmaker." And what a dealmaker he is! Jim has bought and sold over $2 billion worth of businesses in the past several years.[12]

What if Jim's boss hadn't let him go? What if he had told Jim he just needed to buckle down and work harder and he would be an okay HVAC repairman? What if Jim had done that? He would have been trapped in a job that didn't use the potential God gave him. He would have become increasingly miserable in it. By the way, his personality profile pegged him as a developer, i.e. a dealmaker. Just think of the pain and misery that could've been avoided had he known this before he went to school, and if his boss had known it before hiring him. Jim was trapped in a job he didn't fit.

FAIR BUT COMPASSIONATE

First, look at all the possibilities. Sometimes there has been enough growth and change (in the person and/or the organization) that a job can be defined which fits the person and contributes to the objectives of the organization. Usually, though, this isn't the case.

Sometimes there is something in the work environment that can be changed. I have a friend who is really claustrophobic. He needs to sit near a window. Sometimes there is someone the person is working with that is causing a problem; perhaps that person is the one who needs to be dealt with. I have had people on my team that were catalysts for conflict rather than team players.

Sometimes the organizational culture has changed and the employee no longer fits it or agrees with it. If none of these factors can be changed to obtain success in the job, the common sense thing to do is to relieve the pressure from the employee and free them from a situation where they can't be successful or happy. The approaches for dealing with this depend on the answers to some of the questions we asked at the beginning of the chapter. The key is to understand why they don't fit the role. Here are some possibilities and corresponding approaches.

"I MADE A MISTAKE"

I've had occasions where I made a mistake in hiring someone. A couple of times I hired people I thought would work because they had experience even though their personality profile did not fit the role. It did not work our for me, nor have I ever seen an occasion where it worked for anyone else. What do you do in this circumstance? When I came to my senses, I simply admitted my mistake. I sat with the individuals, looked them in the eye, and apologized. I told them that I had done them a great disservice by putting them in a role that did not fit them and that I needed to correct my mistake. I've always been amazed at how well people worked with me when I owned my mistakes.

MY PREDECESSOR MADE A MISTAKE – "I'M SORRY"

Sometimes you make a mistake in hiring and should accept responsibility for it. However, sometimes you are in a more difficult situation: Either predecessors made a mistake in the initial hiring decision, or employees failed to adequately respond to changes that took place since hiring. Either way, you are left to deal with the problem. I've had many times when I had to deal with a predecessor's problem—I'm sure I also left some for my successors to deal with. In this case, don't throw your predecessor under the bus but acknowledge the mistake. Explain to the individual that it works to everybody's benefit to work together and resolve the issue. They need to understand it is better for them, the organization, and the team to deal with the situation rather than to leave it unattended. It's fine to tell them that you personally like them, if that's the case. It's fine to affirm them in any number of ways that you believe are true. Tell them you're sorry they are in this situation and that you hate to be the one dealing with it. But it's your responsibility to do what's best for them and for the organization.

THINGS CHANGED – "IT'S NOT YOUR FAULT"

Many people no longer fit their roles. Given the rapid changes in organizational life, this happens all the time. Organizations are not stagnant entities. The marketplace changes, and the organization changes to meet the needs of the market or its constituents. As this occurs, well-defined roles that individuals used to fit will change.

It can happen in any position. So what do you do? I sit and talk to the affected individual. I'm straightforward but kind and empathetic. I tell them things changed and explain, "You didn't change them. But we both have to respond to the changes." I will point out what has changed that affects their role.

> *"Let no unwholesome word proceed from your mouth,*
> *but only such a word as is good for edification*
> *according to the need of the moment,*
> *so that it will give grace to those who hear."*
>
> *Ephesians 4:29*

I affirm them for their talent and contribution to the organization. Then, I point out that since the position no longer fits their talents and passions, they will be increasingly frustrated and it's not really fair to them, the people who work around them, or the organization. I then begin talking constructively about roles that fit them inside my area, elsewhere in the organization, or outside the organization.

If you leave people in positions they no longer fit, they will cease to be an asset and become a headache.

PEOPLE

Chapter 14

AVOID COMMON PEOPLE MISTAKES

> Thought:
> How much more productivity could you have if you simply avoided the common mistakes leaders often make?

"Where there is no guidance the people fall, but in an abundance of counselors there is victory."
   Proverbs 11:14

"Without consultation, plans are frustrated, but with many counselors they succeed."
   Proverbs 15:22

One of the best ways to get ahead is to avoid decisions that cause you to go backward. This is especially true in the personnel area. Here we look at the key mistakes and how to avoid them.

Mistake # 1 – Keeping underperformers too long

According to Harvey Mackay, you should release a person the first time you think about it.[13] I don't necessarily agree with that, but I do think many leaders wait too long to make a change. While that is benevolent, it is not a good long-term solution. Leaders will wind up giving the rest of the team the short straw, shorting their family, or affecting other important areas of their life. I've seen businessmen in small companies put the wrong people in place and leave them there. It took a heavy toll on their own families, the rest of the business, and their health. I've seen much of the same thing in ministry leaders.

It hurts team morale much more than leaders are usually aware. It makes the other employees less effective in their own jobs and ultimately causes resentment and turnover of the best people. I've seen this happen many times and have caught myself doing it too.

Mistake # 2 – Allowing people to be set up for failure

I'm reminded of a ministry example. A regional ministry growing to a more national scope was expanding to a new city. I saw a personality profile on a city director which I had never seen work in that role and asked about it. The response I got was, "We are trying to force him to grow or get out of the way."

I was appalled! I talked to the national director and I asked, "Would you kick someone on crutches until they either ran or fell over?" He laughed and said, "No." I said, "Isn't that what is happening in this case?" He quickly agreed. We had a good discussion centered on the fact that this was not logical. You don't kick a person on crutches and expect him to run faster. It was not necessary because the situation could be handled in an entirely different way. The person was boxed into a job that didn't fit. We discussed the fact that the ministry's approach to this problem was not fair, nor was it a good spiritual way to deal with this matter. The national director agreed and stated compassionately and honestly that the person was in a role that didn't fit him anymore.

Mistake # 3 – Not being clear about requirements

If you look closely at Scripture, you will have a hard time accusing God of not being clear about His requirements of us. In the very beginning, He gave Adam and Eve great freedom, but He was clear about the one thing that they were not to do. God was equally clear when He gave the Ten Commandments. Four of the ten deal with our relationship with Him and the remaining six deal with our relationship with each other—pretty specific and clear, wouldn't you say? It's very difficult for us to argue that we didn't know what to do or what to avoid. Being clear about the requirements is key to holding people accountable.

Even though we've worked hard to hire the right people and give clear instructions, sometimes course correction is needed. So how are we to handle this? The first thing is to be sure that expectations are clear.

I have had much experience in leading businesses and other organizations where there was a lot of dysfunction, lack of harmony, "firefighting," and, very significantly, mistrust among team members. I remember once leading an organization where one of the support staff was referring to another member of the same team in derogatory terms. I asked, "Why do you think they do a bad job?" I got some general response. Then I asked, "What specific expectation are they not meeting?" I got nothing but silence. This happened many times during that assignment. People repeatedly talked badly about others but couldn't articulate what the agreed-upon expectations were. I see a clear lack of clear expectations in many types of organizations, though it seems to be most prevalent in some non-profits.

As an auditor in a big company, I had a lot of experience with evaluating operations against standards. HCA had operating indicator reports. For everything that was considered of major importance to measure there was a standard, the actual performance, and the difference. Everything we reported as auditors had its basis in some company, industry, or generally accepted accounting standard or principle.

I coached the team to realize that where there is no clear expectation, there is no basis for an expectation gap. Frustration is self-imposed to clear expectations. The person missing the mark the most is the one who has an expectation that is not communicated clearly and agreed upon with the other persons involved.

Mistake # 4 – Holding on to people too long

Sometimes leaders don't deal with people situations as they should simply because since the organization is meeting its objectives they are not forced to deal with them.

Leaders have enough problems to contend with every day, so there's a tendency to deal only with the ones requiring immediate attention. But let's look at this from a stewardship standpoint. Often we are pleased when our teams are making a positive net contribution. For example, let's say the company's desired net profit is 10%. The team celebrates and everyone gets the bonus for delivering 10%. What if the potential of the team was really 20%, 30%, 40%, or even 50%? Should the team be celebrating at 10%? Should the leader receive a bonus? Too often, leaders look at how well they are achieving their target and do not exercise their stewardship responsibilities to optimize what is really possible with the resources available. This is a disservice to the organization and to the other members of the team.

Many tend to think of Jesus as a passive leader who didn't demand a person's best in following Him. Yet at one point in His ministry, Jesus turned to His many followers and urged them to "count the cost" of following Him. The reason He did this was that He expected a total commitment to His calling. We see this point made elsewhere in Scripture, as when Gideon was commanded to let everyone who was afraid go home. His army was eventually whittled down to three hundred fully committed soldiers. In the New Testament, Ananias and Sapphira were struck dead in the church for misrepresenting their commitment. That seems severe to us, but Bible scholars explain that to have allowed this in the early church would have had a substantially negative effect. The same is true in any organization. Half-hearted commitment impacts others.

I will take a very practical example. I go to a number of nonprofit and church gatherings. Some people leading meetings habitually wait for the last few stragglers to come in and, therefore, always start late. I am personally a stickler for showing up on time. But when I am engaged with these organizations, I find myself showing up late because I know the meeting won't start on time anyway. There's a high cost to keeping partially committed people in your organization. There's also a high cost in keeping people in positions where, for whatever reason, they are not doing a good job. Others on the team see it, and either consciously or subconsciously it impacts their commitment and effort. I've experienced this many times.

Mistake # 5 – Not staying on top of change

One of the most common ways a leader can bless people's lives is to make sure that their roles fit their talents and passions. This is not a one-time job; it should be re-evaluated at least annually. As counterintuitive as it seems, sometimes the kindest thing we can do is to begin the process of removing people from roles they do not fit.

Sometimes leaders try to force the fit. Imagine trying to force a piece that doesn't fit the entire puzzle. Does that look very pretty? Of course not. Sometimes, leaders try to carve and reshape the puzzle piece so that it fits. Does it ever work? No! Does this mean that an ill-fitted person can't learn or grow? No, that's not what we are talking about. We're talking about attempting to change the passions and natural giftedness of an individual.

> *"For through the grace given to me, I say to everyone among you not to think more highly of himself than he ought to think; but to think so as to have sound judgment..."*
>
> *Romans 12:3*

One of the things I disciplined myself to do every year was ask if I still fit the role I was in. I would do as honest an evaluation of the issue as I could, but since I realized I couldn't be totally objective, I asked my team and my boss how well they felt I fit my role. I challenged each of my direct reports to do the same thing and had a specific discussion each year on their fit for their role and how any changes were impacting their fit. If I thought I could foresee a time when the role would change and no longer fit them, I had that discussion proactively.

PEOPLE

Chapter 15

HELPING UNDERPERFORMERS

> Thought:
> What is the best way to help underperfomers?

"Treat others the same way you want them to treat you."
Luke 6:31

As I relate the Scripture above to dealing with expectation gaps, I think about what I would want if I was not meeting expectations. Out of thousands of days I showed up for work, there was never a single one when I thought it was okay not to do a good job. And if I were not doing a good job, I would want these things:

- Someone to tell me clearly there was a problem in a way I could understand it.
- An opportunity to resolve the problem and to know what would happen if I couldn't.
- An opportunity to use my talents somewhere else in the organization if I didn't think I could resolve the problem. If that wasn't available, some time and support to find a role in another organization.

My human resources friends at HCA would agree, and their direction was always consistent with this.

Let's think about how God deals with us. He gave us clear instructions through Scripture. He gave us Jesus as an example to follow. Throughout Scripture, He warned His people when they were off track and in the Old Testament sent prophets to explain the consequences of remaining off-track. He was patient in giving His people time to change their ways. He was consistent in delivering the consequences communicated by the prophets. Dealing with people the way God deals with us is generally going to include the following approaches.

BE CLEAR ABOUT WHAT YOU EXPECT

God was always very clear in His instructions to people. The problem was not His instructions but rather their listening and desire to comply. The same cannot be said for many leaders. Many are very scattered, inconsistent, and unclear about what they expect. But they like to blame the resulting problems on their employees.

YOU MAY BE THE PROBLEM

"Therefore encourage one another and build up one another..."

1 Thessalonians 5:11

Chapter 15 – Helping Underperformers

I tend to be a management by exception person. Do you know people who are constantly critical of their staff? I do. There are some leaders that just seem to never be satisfied with the team they have. Some constantly change the team. Some keep their team but constantly complain about them. For these leaders, I have a rather harsh message, "If you want a clear view of the problem, go look in a clean mirror."

> **If nobody is good enough for you, then you aren't a good leader.**

I consulted with one organization where so much had been delegated to one team member—with no clear set of priorities—that he had no idea what to focus on next. Also, things had been delegated to him that did not line up with the strengths of his personality profile. Further, it would have taken two people to do the amount of work delegated to him. Guess what happened? This person who'd been labeled a "hero" two or three years earlier was now labeled a "bad employee" and released.

The release was okay because he did not fit that job or any other the organization had at the time. But the way it was handled was not okay. The problem was not that employee, but the person he reported to. The great irony was that the supervisor was mad at this really good employee. Mistakes the supervisor had made were the real problem.

I consulted for one organization where the leader said, "I'm a great leader. I'm up to the task of coaching a world-class team. The problem is, my team is just not up to par. If the team could do their jobs as well as I can do mine, we would have a world-class organization." Folks, I'm just not creative enough to make up some of the stuff I put in this book. This guy really said that. I stood there dazed, with the words of my daughter going through my head: "Really! Really! Are you kidding me?"

You cannot be a world-class leader and say that you don't have a world-class organization because your team is holding you back. You picked the team or can change it. You train the team and delegate work to them. If there's a problem with the team, you're the problem, not them. And while I'm on a roll, you would be surprised at how many leaders are surprised by that statement.

BE TRUTHFUL

Communicate to the employee kindly, but very plainly, that there is a problem. I've seen employees completely surprised to be terminated for poor performance. When this happens, the greatest failure is on the part of leadership, not the employee. [14]

Unless they know or clearly should have known better, employees should not be terminated until after it has been clearly communicated to them that there is a problem.[15] After an honest discussion, they should be given an opportunity to resign with dignity and find another job or to try to resolve the problem, as long as you think they have a chance to successfully close the expectation gap. Otherwise, give them the opportunity for a graceful exit.

"But speaking the truth in love..."
Ephesians 4:15

Help the employee understand the problem and own the solution. Be as clear as possible about the repercussions of not resolving the problem. Having employed many people over a long career, I've done my fair share of counseling people regarding their performance. People simply don't come to work to do a bad job, and most don't leave work at the end of the day thinking they have done a bad job. In my experience, it has been fairly common for employees who needed counseling to be unaware of the expectation gap. Many times they were ignoring the obvious, but sometimes the expectations weren't as clear as they needed to be for that employee. I tried to help them understand the problem and the need to correct it as clearly as possible.

GIVE THEM A CHANCE TO FIX IT

My Human Resources people suggested that we have the employee create performance improvement plans to solve the problem with specific actions, timeframes, and, most importantly, results. Performance improvement plans should be more for redemptive purposes than just for legal protection. The key is that the employee has to understand that the problem must be solved and that the employee is responsible for the resolution.[16] It's fine and good for the leader to help the employee with the action plan. The trap I have seen many leaders step into, however, is owning the action plan themselves rather than letting the employee own it. Sometimes the employee does the tasks on the action plan, but the problem still exists because the leader did not make clear that the goal was resolution of the problem. The employee needs to own the action plan and the problem.

CLARIFY WHAT HAPPENS NEXT

Be clear at the very beginning of the process about the ramifications of the problem not being solved. Not all problems are termination offenses if not solved. There can be other repercussions to the employee that need to be understood. However, if release will be the consequence, it's especially critical that the employee knows that from the beginning.

You may ask, since a leader's job is to bless employees, how is this a blessing to anyone? Well, let's think about it. Most people I've ever worked with really wanted to do a good job and, while difficult to hear, wanted and needed to know if they were not fulfilling that goal. Good employees appreciate knowing when they're not meeting expectations rather than being talked about behind their backs, or being disappointed at their annual reviews or their raises. They especially want a heads up before they face release or discipline of any kind. Telling people there is a problem is consistent with Paul's instruction to "speak the truth in love." (Ephesians 4:15).

Now the employees are in a position to determine if they can close the expectation gap. If they believe they can't because they don't have the skills or the motivation, they can look for a job while they still have one or resign with dignity and find something they can be successful at.

Giving employees the chance to develop and execute an action plan to solve the problem is as fair as you can be. Being sure they understand the consequences is also being as fair as you can be. Actually, what approach is fairer to the employee and the organization?

I think one reason leaders do not make changes in the organization at all or in as timely a manner as they should is that they are scared of possible legal backlash. I've seen the process just discussed used many times in very difficult circumstances and have seen it be very successful. In about half the cases, the employees were able to solve the problems and continued to grow in their careers and do a good job where they were.

Sometimes employees realized on the front end they either couldn't or wouldn't make the needed changes and resigned. Sometimes, as they worked through the action plan and realized they weren't achieving the results, they began looking for another job, found one, and then resigned.

In my own experience, only about 10%-20% of the people who went through this process ever got to the stage where termination was necessary. Think about it. Taking people through a process that is fair and helps them avoid a termination is a blessing to them compared with what often happens in organizations.

Example

I had just assumed responsibility for a new corporate department, and the vice president in charge told me he had a member on the team that was a problem but that nothing could be done about it. He indicated there were three different sections of labor law that gave this individual protection. My view was this individual did not need protection if he was suited for the job and doing the job. But it would be unfair to the individual to leave him in the job if it wasn't a good fit. We went through the process just described. The individual saw he was not meeting the expectations of the role and that he would not be able to. He found another job outside the company that fit him better and we did not have a lawsuit or any other repercussions from it. If we had not followed this process, I believe we would have had a very different outcome that would not have been constructive for the individual or good for the company.

Chapter 16

INFLUENCE MOTIVATION

> **Thought:**
> How much more could your organization achieve if everyone on the team was highly motivated?

"Whatever your hand finds to do, do it with all your might..."
Ecclesiastes 9:10

Are you confused about why some of your team seems motivated while the rest doesn't? One of the more misunderstood roles of leadership relates to motivation. Walk into any room of leaders/managers and ask them for a definition of motivation. I've always gotten pretty diverse answers. Ask them about their responsibility for motivation, and you get even more diverse opinions. Is the leader responsible for motivating the team? Most people

I've asked say yes. Yet most leaders acknowledge being frustrated by not having a highly motivated workforce.

God intended for us to enjoy our work. In the beginning of creation, work was not drudgery; it was a gift. It's been made difficult by the fall of man, but it is still a gift. So how do we reconcile the command to do our work with all our might and the words of Jesus, "My yoke is easy and my burden is light"? (Matthew 11:30). We can easily work at something with all our might when our heart is in it. What does it take for our heart to really be in our work?

THE ROCK QUARRY

I formed an opinion on this topic before I graduated from collegewhen I was working in a rock quarry during the summers. I made minimum wage and worked long hours in very hot and dusty conditions. But I was genuinely grateful to have the job. I respected and was grateful to the manager, Vernon, who had hired me. My attitude about the job was radically different from some people who were doing the same work for the same pay as I was. In fact, over the course of four summers and doing various jobs around the quarry, I noticed more and more people doing the same work for the same pay and for the same leader, but with really different attitudes and motivation. That's when I decided there's more to this motivation thing than just what the leader does.

So let's break this down and see how motivation really works. We will answer these questions:

- What is motivation?
- Where does it come from?
- What causes it?
- How does the leader influence it?

Why was I motivated to work for minimum wage in a rock quarry? I was raised on a dairy farm. We milked cows twice a day every day. I got up at 4:30 in the morning. We finished the evening milking usually around 6:00 P.M. In the summers, we often worked more after that. I love the fact that I was raised on a farm, and there is much about it that I liked and still miss. But it was not how I wanted to make a living. It was not what I felt called to do. My goal was to work in a business environment. I decided at an early age to take that direction.

There was something inside me that pulled that way. It wasn't someone else's influence but what I wanted that drove me.

As a kid, I thought this was my goal just because I wanted to be cool in the summer and warm in the winter, which the office job offered. It was years later that I discovered my goal was based on far more than that. I have a real passion for organizations and for working with people. Nevertheless, my goals to get a college education and work in business drove me to work hard at the rock quarry and appreciate the opportunity. For me, that job was a means to an end. For some, it was a transitional job. For others, it felt like the end.

Sources of Motivation

I realized from experience that it is possible, and even likely, for leaders to have some people working for them who are motivated while others are not. So I've always been bothered by the number of leadership trainers and written sources that make reference to leaders and their responsibility for motivating people.

Also, I will acknowledge from my own experience that some people in leadership roles universally have highly motivated people while others have universally unmotivated people. I will sort through all of that later. But for my baseline understanding, I went to the Bible to understand motivation. In Scripture, I see three sources of motivation:

- Love
- Desires of the heart
- Pain or fear of discipline

Love

God gave His only son to die for the sins of mankind out of love. In fact, God's motive for everything He does is love; He is love (1 John 4:16). God was not lacking anything. He began creation out of love. The whole Bible is a story of God's love for His people.

Jesus taught His disciples about love. One of His last instructions to them was to love one another. John 15:13 says, "Greater love has no one than this, that one lay down his life for his friends." This teaching was just before His crucifixion, where He would do the very thing He was teaching them.

Love motivates people to do the most amazing things. Parents make amazing sacrifices for their children out of love. I am still astounded at the sacrifices I saw my mom and dad make as they raised six children on a small dairy farm. We did not earn the sacrifices they made, nor did we deserve them. They sacrificed for us out of their love for us. Numerous books have been written on the amazing feats people perform and sacrifices they make out of love for someone in their life.

I deal with leaders in a number of nonprofit ministries. One of the things that distinguishes the most outstanding among them is when their people are serving others from the depths of their hearts out of love. These people do amazing things. Yet it's not only people in nonprofit organizations that have this capacity. There are numerous examples of CEOs, leaders, and others in profitable organizations that also pursue a mission or passion of providing a good or service out of love for the people they are serving. The examples I can think of from my years at HCA are too numerous to mention.

Remember the story about three people laying bricks from the first section of this book? I'm often asked by people in organizations how to get people to move from being bricklayers to builders to cathedral builders. I think the key to this is love. Until people care deeply and passionately about something and someone beyond themselves, they will not likely have the vision of the cathedral builder.

I have listened over the years to some of the great coaches in college athletics. One thing I hear most from some of the greats is how they coach their teams on selflessness, i.e., how much players care about the team and each other versus their own success. I have come to discern by listening to the coaches and watching the teams that the ones who care most about each other have the endurance and put forth the effort to be champions.

So what does this have to do with influencing the motivation of a team? Very simply, people are motivated when you place them in positions where they can do the things they love doing because they love and want to serve others.

It was love that caused Jesus to leave heaven and hang on the cross for us. It was love that caused Moses to tell God to blot him out of His book of life but to spare the children of Israel. It was love that caused Paul to say he would be willing to be eternally damned if only his people would come to know God. And I'm convinced that if you do anything extraordinary, your motivation will be love.

Desires of the heart

Psalm 37:4 speaks of God granting His servants the "desires of your heart." There are many places in Scripture that talk about the desires of the heart. In fact, Proverbs 4:23 says that out of the heart come the "issues of life." What is the heart? It is our seat of decision making, our will, and our emotions. A desire of the heart is simply something that we desire deeply. I can remember when I was a young boy living on the farm, and I wanted a pony. I wanted one so badly that I asked my dad about it every week until he finally gave me one. There was nothing noble or self-sacrificing about this desire. It was just something I wanted deeply enough to keep asking my dad until he decided, out of love, to give it to me.

I remember well when I had a hard time finding an approach to get my teenage son interested in any kind of work. Then one day he started talking about an orange International Scout he wanted to buy. He already had a vehicle I had bought for him that was better than the Scout. I told him that if he wanted the Scout, he should get a job and earn the money to pay for it. He went to work for a landscaping crew and worked really hard all summer to make the money to buy the Scout. At that time, it was a great desire of his heart, and he was willing to do what it took to get it.

With great desire goes great effort. Dan Miller, in *No More Dreaded Mondays*, talks about some things that remind me of this idea of desires of the heart.[17] He says to figure out what makes you mad, glad, or sad. The thinking here is that if something invokes a great emotion in you, such as some injustice that makes you mad or some need of other people that makes you sad or something you want that gives you a deep gladness, you will be highly motivated to act on that emotion.

What do the people on your team care deeply and passionately about? If they are in positions that let them do what they love to do, you will have good solid builders. If they do it for the sake of others, you will have cathedral builders.

The potential for reward is part of this. Peter once told Jesus what he had sacrificed and asked what he would get in return. Jesus did not rebuke him but rather told Peter what he would receive on this earth and hereafter. Jesus often spoke of the rewards of heaven and the punishment of hell. Is it inherently wrong to desire reward for right behavior? No. Nehemiah asked that some of his sacrifices be remembered and rewarded by God.

Discipline/Pain

The final motivation Scripture refers to is discipline or pain. In Deuteronomy 30:15-20 (and surrounding chapters), God outlined His requirements for blessings and also curses that would result if people did not follow His ways. Throughout the Old Testament, God's prophets were sent to His people when they strayed, to warn them of coming judgment if they did not change direction. Judgment or pain was used by God in dealing with His people to change their behavior, but only as a last resort and after much patience.

Now think about this in organizational life. With what type of people do you most frequently need to invoke some discipline or pain? Isn't it the bricklayers? Isn't it the ones there just for the money, just because they need a job? Isn't it all drudgery to them? Remember, what is a drudgery to one person might be a great joy to another who loves to help people.

My suggestion is that if you have people on the team who constantly need discipline, they would be happier in another organization in another role.

THE GREATER THE PAIN THE MORE LIKELY A CHANGE

Country comedian Jerry Clower expresses this idea well. He tells the story of coon hunting with his cousin Marcell. They treed a coon, and Marcell climbed up into the tree to shake it out. He soon discovered they had treed a bobcat, not a coon. The bobcat squalled, and Marcell screamed. This went on for quite some time. Finally, Marcell yelled out to Jerry, "Just shoot up in here amongst us. One of us has got to have some relief." Marcell was a man desperate for something to change. We would say he was highly motivated.

If pain, physical or emotional, causes us to want to change something, are we motivated every time we are in pain? Let's take a common issue for lots of people, myself included. Are you happy with your weight? Are you happy with your overall health and how much you work out? Most people I know would say no. Yet most people are not distressed enough to change. Therefore, we would say they are not motivated. They are just unhappy at this point. Marcell fought with the bobcat for a while before he began experiencing enough pain to tell Jerry to shoot up into the tree.

I'M MISERABLE!

Most people get motivated to go on a diet or start exercising the day they stand in front of a mirror, observe themselves, and either break into tears or (worse) a string of profanities and say something along the lines of "I can't stand this anymore." That level of emotion is usually required to take some action.

When I was a kid, my favorite cartoon was Popeye. In every episode the villain, Brutus, would push Popeye to his limits. Just before Popeye would eat his spinach so that he could be strong enough, he'd say: "I have stands all I can stands, and I can't stands no more." That's when Popeye would take drastic action to make everything right. We tend to be motivated when we can't stand how things are anymore.

ORGANIZATIONAL APPLICATIONS

What does all of this look like in our personal and organizational lives? Brian Tracy would say it is by setting goals that are like heat-seeking missiles. I've always been a goal setter by nature. It comes from my "D"-dominant personality. But Tracy had the earliest and most significant impact on me as a young professional in setting goals and using them in organizational life. I've learned through experience that if you can understand people's goals, you can begin to understand what they do—like my son when he wanted the International Scout. When I helped people set goals they agreed to and believed in, it impacted their performance.

A key to leaders influencing motivation is knowing what people want. Leaders can help illuminate wants and needs that people already have. This is an appropriate thing to do to influence motivation. You might raise this question, "Should we help people want more?" After all, the Bible says to be content with what you have. It says godliness with contentment is great gain (1 Timothy 6:6).

How do we deal with that? The Bible tells us to be content with what we have (Hebrews 13:5). Yet it does not prohibit wanting to do more or have greater impact for God and other people. In fact, it says we are to outdo one another in doing good. I'm reminded of the prayer of Jabez. He asked God to expand his boundaries, and God answered his prayer (1 Chronicles 4:10). Helping people to understand their passions, dreams, goals, and potential in life for God and others is something good leaders should do.

When I led the internal audit department for HCA, I spent considerable time illuminating passions, dreams, and potential goals among the team. Sometimes people's passions and dreams get buried. They've been hurt or failed at some point in life and are just trying to survive, so they put their dreams on hold. Sometimes dreams and passions are ignored or forgotten. People get busy doing what's necessary and forget about doing what they dream about or are passionate about.

Sometimes people just can't see their potential. I spent a lot of time working with people, identifying their potential, and "calling it out" in them. I told them they were setting their sights too low. They didn't have enough self-esteem or enough confidence. Sometimes I pointed people in a different direction because they didn't have good self-awareness.

I don't believe there is such a thing as average, above average, or below average people. People's talents vary, and their effectiveness in using them varies. Therefore, there's average, above average, and below average *performance*. But people are unique. They have specific callings and purposes that God created them for. When people understand and accept their callings, they will be motivated by the desire that springs up within them to live out their callings.

As mentioned before, science tells us God did not create any two snowflakes that are identical. As complicated as the human being is, do we think God ran out of ideas on people? Do we really think people are not unique? Whatever purpose God created people for, they are unique in that purpose and better suited for it than anyone else. Seeing and "calling out" that unique potential in people is a way leaders bless and serve those on their team.

THE LEADER'S ROLE REGARDING MOTIVATION

So, what is the leader's role in motivation? Very broadly, I would say it is to hire people who are already motivated; to help illuminate their passions, dreams, and goals; to help align their goals with the organization's needs; and to try not to de-motivate them. That's easier said than done. How do we accomplish this? It starts with the hiring process. We need to hire people with the following characteristics:

- Right personality profile. If we hire people who are going to be "swimming against the current" of their natural personalities, they will be frustrated and de-motivated from the beginning.

- Right talent and experience. Hire people who want to do the job and know how to do the job.

- Passion and a desire to make a difference— "cathedral builders." I had dinner with an old friend recently who I could tell was really tired. When he described his last few weeks, I understood why. I thought he might be frustrated with his job and ready to quit. Yet that wasn't the case at all. As I listened to him, it was clear he had a great vision for the impact he could have on the company and the quality of healthcare people could receive. He was passionate about making a difference and was willing to push himself to the limits to achieve his goals.

PEOPLE

Chapter 17

INFLUENCE PEOPLE THROUGH HIGH EXPECTATIONS

> **Thought:**
> Have you ever considered how much of your team's and organization's potential you are sacrificing because of your low expectations?

*"Then Jesus said to his disciples,
'If anyone wishes to come after Me,
he must deny himself, take up his cross, and follow Me.'"*

Matthew 16:24

EXPECTATIONS INFLUENCE THE TEAM

Through the experience of having parents and being a parent, I know firsthand the impact of expectations on people. In my family, we were expected to work hard. We did, and it just seemed normal. In my wife's family, they did a lot of things to please and meet the expectations of other people. That thinking was so ingrained in her that she still does it to this day. When I ask her why she's doing something, her response is often based on what somebody else expects. The expectations I had of my children has impacted them significantly. I talked in an earlier chapter about how I guided them in college based on their hard-wiring.

In society I see the impact of expectations on people. There are for-profit businesses and nonprofit organizations that have cultures of high expectation. By contrast, there are those that have cultures of low expectation resulting in mediocrity.

Sadly, I see this in the church in North America. Many churches have cultures of low expectations. Frankly, the standard required to be involved in a social fraternity or sorority in college is higher than that required to be a member of many churches.

The importance of teacher expectations in facilitating student learning has long been recognized.[18] What you believe about people drives your attitude toward them. Your attitude drives your communications with them and your behavior toward them. That in turn drives their attitude and behavior. They start reacting to you through either positive or negative attitude and behavior.

The first psychologist to systematically study this phenomenon was a Harvard professor named Robert Rosenthal in an elementary school south of San Francisco.[19] Many years ago, an experiment was done in a school in the San Francisco Bay area. The principal told three teachers that they were the best teachers in the system. He also told them that they would be given ninety high IQ students. At the end of the year, the students had achieved 20% to 30% more than other students in the area. The surprise came when the principal called the three teachers and told them they did not have gifted students. He had randomly selected the students. He also told the teachers that they were not selected because of their superior skills but were randomly selected as well. [20]

Chapter 17 – Influence People Through High Expectations

If you expect something to happen, you increase the chances of its happening. If you expect something good to happen, you tend to be optimistic, you look for opportunities, and you set goals. Over time, with this outlook of preparedness, chances greatly increase that something good *will* happen.

Conversely, when you expect something bad to happen, you are pessimistic, you miss opportunities, and you behave in a way that generally does bring some disappointment to your life. This is true even in the area of health. The medical field established long ago that people with positive and expectant attitudes are healthier and live longer than those with negative and depressed ones.

REINFORCE WHAT YOU EXPECT

In college, we studied the work of Pavlov and how he trained dogs. Positive and negative reinforcement is used in all animal training. Let's end the discussion of motivation on a positive note by talking about how to get the behavior you need from people. You may remember better by thinking of Pavlov and the slobbering dogs. All animal training is done using a simple approach: You give positive reinforcement to behaviors or actions you want to see repeated (carrot) and negative reinforcement to actions or behaviors you do not want to see repeated (stick/pain). When animals are trained, each movement in the right direction is rewarded with food. Over time, the animals must do more and more to receive their food.

People are not animals and shouldn't be treated like animals. But positive and negative reinforcement can be used in organizational life to get the behaviors you want and to see that certain behaviors are avoided. That is, as long as it's done in the proper way with the right motivations. This is consistent with the biblical idea of accountability.

Let us look at some examples. Suppose you want to encourage teamwork among your employees. There are some on your team that like public recognition, but they tend to operate independently. If the leader acknowledges them in public when they contribute to a team effort in the appropriate way, those individuals will tend to repeat similar type behaviors to get the recognition. Be careful with this because not all people like public recognition. Some people most appreciate a pat on the back, a warm thank you or a personal note from the leader to repeat a behavior.

If you're trying to create a culture that follows the biblical instruction to "go the extra mile" (Matthew 5:41), every time people do something extra, reward them in some way that's meaningful to them. I found that oftentimes a simple gift certificate for a meal will substantially impact employees' desires to look beyond just the immediate of what they have to do. I would add, however, to keep this in balance so that employees do not start neglecting family or other important goals in life by responding to your positive reinforcement.

I remember Steve, the "straw boss" I worked for in the summer as a teenager. Each year, we hauled hay on the farm where Sydney worked. Sydney was pretty much a loner and didn't get much attention, but he was quite strong. Each day, he would come by and throw a few bales of hay. Steve would start bragging on him. The more Steve bragged, the harder Sydney would work until he was literally exhausted. And Steve wasn't paying Sydney. He was doing it purely for the recognition. It is often amazing to me how badly people need attention and positive reinforcement. I noticed over the course of my career that solid leaders who make a habit of positive reinforcement have lower turnover and much more loyal and content employees. Positive reinforcement brings blessing to people's lives because it is such a strong need. This is an area where I had some good moments but a lot more that I'm not proud of. I missed a lot of opportunities to bless people by encouraging them.

How about negative reinforcement?

But, you may ask, what about negative reinforcement? You probably heard it said, "Praise in public, chew in private." Generally, I favor that approach. But is it an absolute? When Jesus was telling His disciples what would happen to Him, Peter argued with Him. Jesus said in front of the other disciples, "Get behind me, Satan." (Matthew 16:23). That was a pretty strong rebuke, wouldn't you say? It would've been strong in private, but it seemed especially strong in front of the other disciples. Why did Jesus do that? Was it because He did not like or respect Peter? No, because another time Jesus said to him, "You are Peter, and on this rock I will build my church." (Matthew 16:18a NIV). Jesus handpicked him to be the leader of the disciples when He was gone. Jesus' rebuke was strong because Peter was making a huge spiritual mistake which Jesus did not want to see him repeat, nor did He want the other disciples to repeat it.

Public rebukes can be done at the wrong time, in the wrong way, and with the wrong motivation and can be very destructive to people. However, they can also be significant learning opportunities for the individual and others. So negative reinforcement with love is also a part of the leader's playbook. In the home, psychologists often refer to this as "tough love." The form of negative reinforcement needs to fit the individuals who need to change their behavior.

WHAT IS YOUR ATTITUDE TOWARD PEOPLE?

I know I guy who is a fine Christian leader. He is admired by his family, respected by the community, and loved by his peers. But he is disliked by his employees. He shared his concern with me about how his employees view him. I began asking questions about his relationships in every other area of life and he confirmed that they were healthy and positive. Then I asked him the key question, what was the difference in how he viewed all the other people in his life that respected, admired, and loved him and the employees in this company that disliked him. He came down to one simple thing: his attitude.

He is very accepting of and loving toward the people in all other spheres of life. He sees himself as a servant and people as individuals he can serve. He serves well—kindly, gently, and respectfully. The people respond positively.

But somehow his view of employees in his company is different. He said, "In my company, I see myself as the boss, the one to be served, and I see the employees as the ones who are supposed to serve me." I asked what else he thought about the employees. I already knew because I had heard him articulate frustrations over a long period of time. The truth is, he saw them as lazy, dishonest, and, in general, not as productive as he wanted them to be.

I contrast this leadership to what I saw at HCA under Dr. Frist Jr. He was an optimist. He believed in and expected the best out of people. He believed he was wrong about his view of them only when somebody proved him wrong, usually more than once. He was generous and shared wealth through stock options with people. As a result, he blessed more people financially than anybody else I know. I pause and think about how different the culture would have been and how different the results would have been if his attitude had been different. Both Dr. Frist and the other leader got mostly what they expected of their teams in the end.

Any time I can understand a person's attitude toward other people and know their personality profile, I can predict with a degree of accuracy how they're going to respond to people and especially how they're going to respond to people when they are under pressure.

There's a Scripture that says that whatever you sow, that you will also reap (Galatians 6:7). This is true in all areas of life, but especially in leadership. If you expect people to be talented, hard-working, and honest, some will disappoint you, but many will live up to your expectations. By contrast, if you expect people to be lazy, dishonest, and non-productive, then a few people might pleasantly surprise you, but most are going to meet your expectations. That's not necessarily because that's "how they are." They are reacting to your attitude and interactions with them. A leader with that attitude cannot and does not treat people with the dignity and respect they deserve, and the people react to that negatively.

I know another guy that didn't have the culture or relationship with employees he wanted. He's a fine Christian man and a good leader. I probed him about his attitude toward employees. He's a very social and engaging individual, but much to my surprise, I found out that he generally didn't trust his employees. I asked him why he hired people he couldn't trust. He indicated he thought he had good people, but just had a trust issue. He dealt with this issue spiritually and changed his attitude toward the people that worked for him. Within a year, God had blessed him and his employees in significant ways. They were all happier and the company's bottom line was much healthier.

If I can understand your attitude toward people, I can understand your actions and reactions to them and actions and reactions toward you. What Scripture says is true: whatever you sow, you also reap.

My personality profile says I tend to expect people to be better than they can be. That's negative in the sense that I expect too much out of people. There's also a positive aspect of this though. I expect great things from people. I expect people to do well and accomplish much. As I look back over my career, I think many times people were better than they would have been and better than they thought they could be because I believed they could do great things. In fact, many of them did. As I reflect, I'm humbled and grateful to have been allowed to lead such a great group of people.

I'm not recommending that you act like an ostrich and put your head in the sand to ignore bad behavior or ignore a person of bad character. You do so at

Chapter 17 – Influence People Through High Expectations

your own peril. I'm saying that generally your attitude drives how your people are going to respond to you.

MAKING A DIFFERENCE – FRANK'S STORY

A young boy once brought a Christmas present to school for his teacher, Mrs. Jones. She opened her gifts in front of the students. When she opened Frank's gift, the other kids laughed. It was a partially used bottle of perfume. Frank was obviously embarrassed because of the laughter of the other kids, but Mrs. Jones thanked him for it and made over it like it was a fine gift even though she didn't quite understand.

A bit later when none of the other students were around, Mrs. Jones asked Frank how he chose that particular gift. Tears came to his eyes as he explained that it was his mom's perfume. He had given it to his mom last Christmas because he knew it was her favorite perfume. His mom was very sick that Christmas, but she always wore it and thanked Frank for it. She passed away a few months later. Frank told Mrs. Jones that he hoped she liked it as much as his mom did and wanted her to have it so she would smell like his mom.

> *"Do not look out merely for your own personal interests, but also for the interests of others."*
> *Philippians 2:4*

Mrs. Jones then took a special interest in Frank. She found out about his home life, which was tough. His father did the best he could but was poor and had to work long hours, leaving Frank to fend for himself. Mrs. Jones began to look at Frank differently. She determined she would encourage, support, and love him. In the final half of his fourth-grade year, Frank went from being a poor student to a very good student. In the years that followed, Frank would always go by and see Mrs. Jones every year and tell her how he was doing. He was making As every year. At some point he moved away, and she didn't see him anymore.

A few years later, she got a note from Frank. He had just graduated from high school with honors, and he wrote a note to Mrs. Jones thanking her for the difference she had made in his life. Four years later, she got another note from Frank. He had just graduated from college at the top of his class. A few years later, she got another note thanking her for the impact the she had on his life. He had just finished medical school and was now a doctor.

It's amazing how much impact you can have on a person's life by investing your time in them and having high expectations.

Chapter 18

DELEGATE EFFECTIVELY

> **Thought:**
> How much better would your quality of work life be if you could delegate anything you do to other people and be confident it would be done well?

*"Moses' father-in-law said to him,
'The thing you're doing is not good.
You will surely wear out, both yourself and
these people who are with you, for the task
is too heavy for you; you cannot do it alone.'"*

Exodus 18:17-18

What's the first decision any leader has to make? There are two approaches we learn from Moses and Jethro, his father-in-law. Moses kept all of the work to himself, and people were gathered all around him looking for answers. Jethro's approach, which Moses later adopted, was to delegate to capable leaders and handle only the harder cases himself.

In my experience, three simple keys to effective delegation are to be sure the person to whom you assign a task:

- Wants the assignment.
- Understands the assignment.
- Knows how to complete the assignment.

Do they want this assignment?

Sometimes, people know how to do something, but they simply don't have any interest in doing it—there's no passion.

Do they understand?

It sounds so simple, doesn't it? You just tell people what to do. They are eager to please the boss, so they smile and nod. If you ask them whether they understand, they are likely to say yes whether they do or not. They don't want you to think they are not smart, and they are hoping they can figure it out.

It has been my experience that the delegation process breaks down in telling people what you want them to do. Why is that? It's because it's a complicated process.

The internal audit department at HCA was staffed with young, bright, hardworking professionals. They were very eager to please. They were very hesitant about saying they did not understand. They normally would smile and say they understood. If they didn't understand, they would wait until I left and hope that a more experienced person on the team could explain. After a few experiences, I learned to look deep into their eyes. I could discern a look of comprehension, or I would see what I called a "dazed" or "glazed" look. When I saw this, I knew they did not understand. Sometimes, I would say, "Tell me the first thing you will do to complete this assignment." Seldom did they know. Then I would go over it again and sometimes yet again until I was confident they understood what they were to do. If they can explain to you the objective of the job and a general approach for accomplishing it, they likely understand.

Do they know how?

Sometimes, people simply don't know how to do the task you are assigning. I faced this often in the internal audit department. The answer to this is simple: Either do it yourself, give it to someone else, or train someone.

DELEGATION PITFALLS

When my people complained, I tried to listen to what they thought should be changed or improved and gave related projects to those individuals if I felt they had the competence. This approach did three things. First, it got the work done by someone who cared about it. Second, it stopped a lot of complaining. Third, it reinforced the culture of not complaining about something unless you were willing to fix it. It's important for people to do something they believe in and care about. Ecclesiastes says, "Whatever your hand finds to do, do it with all your might."(Ecclesiastes 9:10). This is an encouragement to work hard at whatever we do whether we like it or not. I don't consider myself an author, but I thought of that Scripture many times while writing this book.

On the other hand, Jesus said, "My yoke is easy and my burden is light." (Matthew 11:30). So how do these two ideas work together? Leaders must give people work assignments they have the talent, experience, and passion for rather than giving them assignments that are drudgery for them. One business owner I know keeps giving people tasks they aren't even qualified for.

Though writing is not my favorite thing to do, God gave me years of experience and practice at doing it, and He gave me great passion for things I can do once this book is written. What I will be doing in the future will be made much easier because God had me write this book.

Delegation is important. Without it, you can't grow your staff and organization or increase your span of control. But there are some pitfalls you need to be aware of because they can cause you some big problems. These problems arise from ignoring teachings of Scripture in this area:

- Know the condition of your flock. — Proverbs 27:23
- Don't lord it over them. — Matthew 20:20-28
- "My yoke is easy and my burden is light." — Matthew 11:28-30

Know the condition of your flock

This command certainly can apply to knowing the status of your organization or business. It also means knowing what your people can handle. I have heard many leaders over the years describe what I consider a reckless approach to leadership. They say, "My approach is just to throw them in over their heads and let them sink or swim." I have seen leaders do that many times. The problem is sinking people tend to take others down with them, including the leader that threw them in.

I've seen the "throw-them-in-over-their-head" approach used many times. The "I" and "I"/"D" personalities are most prone to doing this. When people are hired, or existing people receive a new assignment, often the leader just gives a free rein and lets people go do it. You say, "So what's wrong with that?" Well, you hire people believing they have a certain level of competence and motivation. But you've done absolutely nothing to validate or test that belief. The justification is "They are professional, and I pay them well. Therefore, I just need to trust them." And certainly, it's true that employees do need to feel like you have confidence in them.

On the other hand, it is also true their confidence can erode, and people can get frustrated with micromanagers that never really let go and give them autonomy.

Don't lord it over them

I understand this command to be telling us to avoid being abusive or overly controlling. People need and thrive on freedom when they are doing something they know how to do and have a passion for. When we are overly controlling, we limit people and restrict their freedom—and ours as well. It takes time and energy to look over someone's shoulder. When we don't empower people properly in the delegation process, we limit ourselves as well.

You don't have to choose between throwing people in and seeing if they can swim and looking over their shoulders all the time. There is a third alternative which will get the best results. It is a balanced approach. You give them freedom after you know what they can do. One way to know this is by verified experience. The other is by observing them. Employees need to be fully immersed in meeting the objectives of the organization. They need to be part of something where they maintain their distinctiveness but contribute fully to the whole. This need requires their being fully immersed in the job you have given them but not in over their heads. In this approach, you give them responsibility and authority in smaller steps.

I hired a subcontractor recently to do some work at my house. He had just previously hired a worker who described his skills in a particular area of work that this subcontractor had never actually seen him do. He threw this new hire in "over his head" and sent him to my house unsupervised. The person messed up the job.

Using a balanced approach avoids a lot of mistakes and saves a lot of time correcting problems for the new employee and yourself. Consider the example I just gave. It cost this contractor considerable money to fix the problems caused by his employee. In addition, he risked not getting any future business from me, plus losing the potential for referrals that I would have given. This was a very costly mistake for the individual that easily could have been avoided. The cost of some additional supervisory time would have been minimal compared to what it cost him to throw this employee in "over his head."

Make this transition for new people as quickly as possible but not until you have a clear understanding of their capabilities. You avoid much of the frustration new employees may feel in being micro-managed by explaining your approach. In doing so, the employees know your intent is to let go but not drop them in over their heads. It's best to solicit the cooperation of the employees to make the transition as quickly as possible.

If you drop the new employees in over their heads, they're going to take on some water that wasn't necessary. But when you walk them into the water up to their chins, they are fully immersed in the ownership of the project or task, but not drowning. This is the optimal place for the employers and the employees to be. It's like a river. A drop of water is completely a part of the river but retains its distinctiveness. Individuals need to be fully immersed in their role but maintain their uniqueness.

The approach above is consistent with how Jesus led His disciples. First, He taught them. Then, He did things in their presence like healing people. Then, He sent them out in two's and had them come back and report on the results.

"My yoke is easy, and my burden is light"

Since God never intended for people to be overloaded and burdened in their work, leaders should not overburden them either.

How many times do you find that people have more projects than they have time to complete? Do they put off one project and do the others? Or do they spread the time they have among all the projects? What is the result? One project dies from neglect, or all the projects suffer due to insufficient time and attention. The results can be devastating because all the projects may fail.

What's the better approach? Prioritize the projects. Are all equally time sensitive? Sometimes they are not. Are all equally important? Generally they are not. Under such circumstances, the leaders and employees should agree on which project gets deferred or dropped altogether. Otherwise, a high-priority project could die from neglect, or multiple important projects could be done poorly due to insufficient time and attention.

DON'T OVERLOAD YOUR BEST PEOPLE

I can see two principles related to delegation covered in this Scripture. One is that when people are doing work they were designed for, it tends to be easy for them. Coupled with the numerous commands in Scripture about rest, I also take this to mean that people should not be overloaded. Overloading hurts individuals, but it also hurts leaders. When leaders overload people, they position themselves to become overly dependent on an individual or a few individuals. The unintended consequences of ignoring this Scripture can be significant.

> *"For in six days, the Lord made the heavens and the earth, the sea and all that is in them, and rested on the seventh day; therefore the Lord blessed the Sabbath day and made it holy."*
>
> *Exodus 20:11*

In organizations, delegation is sometimes like water: It follows the path of least resistance. Some people are eager to take on more and more work. So what's the problem? You can become overly dependent on key individuals. This naturally tends to happen in small organizations but will also happen in larger ones if you are not careful.

I know of a businessman in Nashville who had a quite successful small business. He had one person responsible for his billing and accounts payable. That individual got sick. Customers were not being billed, so his cash flow was cut off. Vendors were not being paid and were upset. It caused a substantial disruption in his business for a period of time. If this had continued, it could have ruined his business. A great many business owners or leaders, as well as non-profit leaders, have had a similar experience.

One key rule of wise investing is diversification—in other words, don't put all your eggs into one basket. This applies to many aspects of organizational life, like not being overly dependent on one customer or supplier. It also applies to your people: Don't become overly dependent on a few key people.

It's not uncommon for leaders to brag on who they think are the very best people in the organization and the best fits for their jobs when, in fact, these people are dangerous to the long-term success of the organization. This idea is counterintuitive, so we need to unpack it. Picture an employee who works hard (doing the work of two or three people), and whom you count on enormously. Most leaders think everything is right about the situation. They say, "I don't know what I would do without Mary." And that's the essence of the problem. What would you do without Mary?

The implication is quite simple. If something happens to your special person, you are in a real jam. But you say they aren't going anywhere. Do they never take vacation? Do they never get sick? Are they never going to retire? Are they not someday going to get promoted or transferred? If they are so good, is it not possible that someone would offer them a better package and hire them away from you? The reality is that it's not *if* you lose them, it's simply when and how. If you truly don't know what you would do without them, you need to start figuring out now what you will do when they are gone.

Jesus' work was too important to not be passed on or have a backup plan when something happened to one of his followers. His plan was the one Paul shared with Timothy:

> *"The things which you have heard from me*
> *in the presence of many witnesses,*
> *entrust these to faithful men (people)*
> *who will be able to teach others also."*
> *2 Timothy 2:2*

There are some alternatives. You can hire someone else and split up the work. This is difficult, particularly in small organizations. Another alternative is to train one or more people on everything like we did in internal audit. Then you have a backup when something happens. Again, this is hard in a small organization. Another alternative is to have a documentation file on how each person does their job. We did this in internal audit due to the high turnover. That way, at least someone can be trained using the documentation to fill the role more quickly.

Of course, the best solution is to plan and delegate in a way that avoids this problem from ever occurring. This is often easier said than done, especially in smaller organizations. Let's consider a typical scenario. The organization is having some success in its new business. Therefore, there is more work to do. Mary sees this as an opportunity to gain favor with the boss and have more impact and influence in the organization. She says, "I'll pick up the extra work." She does, and the boss is very appreciative. This keeps happening, and eventually the boss starts thinking about adding an employee. Mary wants to gain more favor with the boss to have influence in the organization and to provide more financially for her family. She says, "Don't hire anybody else. I will just work more and you can pay me more." That sounds like a good deal to the boss. So that is what the boss does. As this continues over time, the organization becomes too dependent upon Mary.

My computer expert

Let me tell you about Marty. This guy was a computer whiz. The company had an information technology department with hundreds of employees. I would ask them about the project for my department, and they might say it would take six weeks. But Marty could consistently do the project in two weeks. I was proud of Marty, bragged about him, and paid him well. I had begun to say, "I don't really know what I would do without him."

Then it dawned on me, someday somebody would see how good Marty really was and that "somebody" would hire him away from me. Then what would I do? So we changed Marty's goals. One of his goals was to write new programs. Another related to documenting very well how to operate programs already written so that any programmer could come in and maintain, improve, or change those programs. Doing this served us very well when this function grew and we hired someone else. Very quickly, they were able to carry on and even expand on the base of what we had already developed because of the documentation and training that we had Marty write and implement.

Chapter 19

CREATE A CULTURE THAT EMPOWERS

> Thought:
> Have you considered how many people stay with your organization because they like the culture or how many leave because they don't like it?

"Brethren, join in following my example, and observe those who walk according to the pattern you have in us."

Philippians 3:17

An organization's culture is, in essence, the values of its top leaders put into action. The values of leaders are expressed through mission, vision, objectives and goals, policies, and procedures, but they are most clearly expressed by the attitudes and actions of the senior leadership team. The

Apostle Paul encouraged people to follow the example he was setting for them. Since values are lived out by key leaders, let's look at some examples.

Key values

Many years ago, I wrestled with the values needed for leading organizations. During my leadership of the internal audit department at HCA, I developed what I called the internal audit success profile. These were the five characteristics I saw in people who got promoted or who went on to other parts of the organization and excelled. These five characteristics were service, innovation, teamwork, communication, and continuous learning. Your culture is driven by your values in action.

Over time, I noticed these weren't just the characteristics of successful individuals, but they were characteristics of successful departments and organizations. I refined and developed the items on my list into value statements. Later, I felt the need to add a sixth characteristic, integrity, to the list. In the internal audit department, integrity seemed to go without saying, but in other places it needed to be said.

> **Integrity** — This means doing the right thing for the organization and other people regardless self-interest. It's doing what is right when nobody's looking. It's doing what is right just because it's the right thing. If people don't trust you to have their interests in mind or the organization doesn't trust you to have its interests in mind, why would or should you be trusted to serve in any capacity?
>
> **Service** — This is adding measurable value to the other person or the organization. There are two kinds of people in the organization: those who want power and want others to serve them as their primary aim, and those who want to add value to others and the organization. People seeking power make poor servants.
>
> I was able to predict the demise of several corporate initiatives because I saw the primary aim of the leadership in charge was to gain power. Invariably when that was the case, the initiative or function ultimately was disbanded. Unfortunately, it usually took much longer for this to happen than it should have.
>
> **Innovation** — Because things change and our expectations are always for something better in the future, we have to be creative to continue to provide higher levels of service. If we don't work

at providing higher levels of service, someone else will, and we will become obsolete.

Teamwork — There is an old saying, "None of us are as smart as all of us." Proverbs says there is wisdom in many counselors (Proverbs 11:14, 15:22). There is great value in avoiding mistakes through gaining the perspective of others. I found over many years that people working together are more creative and innovative for the organization than individuals are.

The Physician Services organization at HCA evolved over twelve years from having a very narrow focus to having many initiatives and functions. The ideas came from many individuals to help the organization evolve and improve. But no matter who had the initial idea, it was always improved upon by the team.

Communication — When God wanted to halt the progress of mankind as they built the tower of Babel, He made them speak different languages so they could not communicate effectively. When teams are not committed to proactive communication, many problems arise. When I speak of communication, I don't simply mean talking. I mean deliberate and meaningful communication where there is a meeting of the minds.

Where there is not good communication, there cannot be good teamwork. Where there is not good teamwork, there cannot be good innovation. Where there is not good innovation, there cannot be improved service. In addition, where there is not good communication, your integrity can even be questioned.

Continuous learning — To create a product or provide a service, everyone involved must bring some skill to the table. Given the rapid rate of change in the world, a commitment to lifelong learning is key to continuing to contribute to a high-performance team.

These became the values I tried to live by and incorporate into the value statements of each organization I led at HCA, and they served the team well in the healthcare business. If you can't clearly articulate your values, they aren't clear to the team.

Do you know the culture you have?

Different cultures may be needed based on the nature of the business organization. For example, technology organizations may need a more competitive internal culture, more accepting of some lone rangers because of their technical expertise. In certain healthcare situations, absolute teamwork is a required and necessary part of the culture.

Vision, priorities, accountability systems, policy and procedures, and the attitudes and actions of the top leaders all impact the organization's culture. Often cultures are not understood by leaders driving them. Very frequently, the leaders don't appreciate the value a healthy culture brings, or the damage that is typically done when the culture is not what it should be. Often the culture is not what the leaders think it is or want it to be. Their value statements and policies regarding people say one thing, such as "People are our most valuable asset; we value and respect our people," yet the leaders act differently. They may not treat people as though they value or respect them. They may think of them more as an expense item on the income statement and treat them accordingly.

Or, the leaders may say they value families, yet work sixty to eighty hours a week themselves and expect the same from others. It's not uncommon for males to think that working hard and providing well proves they value their families. However, it is time and involvement with family activities that make the spouse and children believe that they are valued. I have seen cultures that talk significantly about family values and say all the right things but model the opposite. Culture attracts people to your organization or causes them to want to leave.

Is the leadership team modeling the values?

Sometimes, the leaders model the right behavior but include people on their senior leadership team that don't. I recall an instance where the earnest desire of the senior leadership team was to treat people as valuable and with respect. However, one person was included on the senior leadership team that didn't buy into that value. That person treated people horribly. Everyone knew it and despised the person. The worst part, though, was the impact it had on the culture and on the credibility of the top leaders. It was seen as hypocritical and completely meaningless when the top leaders talked about how much they valued people and wanted people treated with dignity.

I regret to say that I've done this myself. I wanted a culture that was very heavily oriented toward teamwork. I had bright and hard-working technical people around me that I felt were needed to accomplish certain goals for the team. Yet they didn't believe in teamwork, or at least view it the same way I did and in the way others needed to experience it. No matter what I did, the culture I wanted and the culture I was seeing were different until I made the hard decisions. I had to replace hard-working technical people with sometimes less talented, more team-focused people. Every time I made those concessions, though, we upped the morale and the overall results of the team improved because of the synergy we got from everybody working together. Employees went the extra mile because they enjoyed what they were doing and the people they were doing it with.

PEOPLE

Chapter 20

LEAD CHANGE

> Thought:
> What potential are you giving up by not being proactive in leading change?

"... but one thing I do: forgetting what lies behind and reaching forward to what lies ahead."

Philippians 3:13

Dick Wells, author of *Sixteen Stones*, says the difference between your present position and your vision is the change that is necessary to achieve your desired future.[21] One thing we all deal with in organizational life is change. My experience has been that the initial reaction to change is either skepticism or outright resistance unless people are already clamoring for change. Some leaders avoid making changes until they have to because of the tendency of some people not to like change.

Auditors tend to be more comfortable with the status quo. I would get some resistance every year when we made our plans and plotted changes. I would ask, "Do you want a year with no change?" Most of them said yes. I said "Are you sure?" And they said, "Yes." I said, "Let me remind you, no change means no compensation increases, or promotions." They quickly said, "No, we want *those* changes."

I applied the idea to the broader company, showing that if we didn't change anything to continue to grow profits, there would not be money for merit or promotional increases. When the team understood that change was necessary for progress, they were open to it.

A LEADER'S ROLE IN THE CHANGE PROCESS

A critical role of leadership in an organization is to lead change efforts. It can be frustrating because it's not easy. It tends to cause tension, and many times the improvement sought is not achieved. Why is there so much tension and resistance if change is necessary for progress, which people tend to want?

CHANGE IS UNCOMFORTABLE AND INEFFICIENT

Change isn't comfortable for many people. It's especially uncomfortable for certain personality types that do a lot of the work in organizations. Plus, change is initially inefficient. You may ask how change can lead to progress if it's inefficient. Change is like taking one step backward and two steps forward. In fact, that is the picture of a successful change. An unsuccessful change is like two steps backward and one step forward. A neutral change is one step backward and one step forward.

Leaders often have ideas for improvement. It's very clear to them that the change will be an improvement over the old way of doing things. They get excited about the impact of their new idea. It's such a good idea that they forget some people tend not to like change. Then, when people *don't* wholeheartedly embrace the change, they get upset.

Leaders need to remember that people take a while to adapt to changes—even good ones. Remember the children of Israel in the Bible. Moses led them out of slavery, and they were free people. What did they do almost immediately? They began to complain. There were aspects of their enslaved lives that they remembered and missed. Even though the change was positive, living through the change seemed hard.

It's common to see this with computer conversions. People will beg and almost cry for better technology. The new software is implemented. Now, the screens and reports don't look the same. Even though they may be better, it takes longer to do what the employees used to do. It's not long before people are literally crying and wishing they had the old system back.

How not to lead change

Let me tell you what doesn't work. Early in my career, I had just assumed leadership responsibilities for the internal audit department at HCA. The culture, the processes, and the results all needed to change. The department needed to gain more credibility, and it needed to happen within the next year. I locked myself away in my office for a few days, including some weekend time. I came up with goals that I saw as critical to what we needed to accomplish in the next year.

I called a meeting of my direct reports and proudly laid out the goals and initiatives that we would need to accomplish. I waited for my team to respond, expecting them to be impressed with the thoroughness of my work and the soundness of the plans, and to have a great deal of appreciation for the fact that I figured all this out for the team without making them do it. It seems so foolish now, but I was genuinely surprised at their near rebellion. It wasn't that they didn't think the plans were good; they were simply overwhelmed by them. Being a new leader, I did the only thing I could think of. I retreated!

I asked them what they thought were the most important changes we needed to make. They told me. I asked them what we could get done in the next month. We wrote it down and agreed. I asked which of the proposed changes we could make in the next week. We wrote those down and agreed. We did this every week for a month and, at the end of the month, had accomplished more than we thought we could do that first month.

We went through the process for another month. We made plans weekly and monitored progress. At the end of the second month, we had accomplished more that we had targeted for the month.

Now I could see the team was gaining momentum. So we tried the same process again, but this time we set goals for the next three months. We monitored progress monthly. At the end of three months, we had exceeded the goals we set. We continued to do this for the balance of the year. At the end of the year, we had accomplished more than the goals and initiatives I had initially outlined.

THE KEYS TO LEADING CHANGE

Involve the team

People like to have a say in change that affects them. We all know that from our own experience. They're much more accepting of change they help plan. Nehemiah was masterful at this (Nehemiah 2:17-18). When people have input and involvement in making the plans and setting the deadlines, they feel ownership and commitment that doesn't exist when plans are simply announced. Plus, you usually avoid a lot of unintended consequences, and you get better ideas by having everyone involved. Remember, the "S" and "C" temperaments are going to see unintended consequences that the "D" and "I" temperaments don't.

We can take a cue from Jesus. He wants to change our lives and change them radically. Yet in Revelation 3:20 we read, "Behold I stand at the door and knock. If anyone hears my voice and opens the door, I will come in…" Think about this. If the creator of our universe waits for an invitation to come in and change us, shouldn't we think long and hard about forcing people to change? It's much better to invite and lead change than to force it.

Set goals the team believes are achievable

The team was simply overwhelmed with the goals I laid out for the year. By contrast, Nehemiah only asked the people to build the wall six inches per day.[22] Time proved that my plans were achievable because we accomplished even more. But my plans were more than the team could absorb at the time. People's experiences and personality profiles determine the timeframes in which changes need to be accomplished. Some personalities can get overwhelmed. Others tend to set goals too high. Some leaders, knowing that people tend to fight change, assume the only way or best way to make it is to force it and get it over with. That does work sometimes, but you always pay a price for it, and it's very risky. You don't know how people will respond. Sometimes a forced change at work is the "straw that breaks the camel's back." They may have already accumulated a lot of baggage and pent up emotions.

When team members respond negatively to pressure or a perceived threat, it's wise to quickly sit with them and try to understand what else is going on in their lives. Most of the time, I found their behavior or attitude was driven by something going on in their lives other than work circumstances. By understanding that, we could avoid some damaged relationships and problems in our organization downstream.

Share the credit

I noticed in the eighth chapter of Nehemiah that after the wall-building project was completed, he called a great gathering of the people. Yet unlike many leaders who would call such a gathering and take credit for success and maybe share some of the credit with their key leaders, Nehemiah brought no attention to himself at all. Rather, he put the priests in charge of the event. They celebrated their success. Nehemiah acknowledged the work of every group of people. He didn't brag on the top performers. He acknowledged the amount of work they all did, and he didn't criticize the ones who did the least. Rather, he acknowledged what they did to contribute to the success of the whole project. Nehemiah didn't take any of the credit. He didn't seek the approval or accolades of the people. He only asked for one thing. He asked God to remember his service and sacrifice.

Mustard seed and leaven (yeast) approach

God's approach to making changes is quite simple. From the parable of the mustard seed in Matthew 13:31, we see the importance of starting small and letting something grow over time. From the parable of the leaven, in Matthew 13:34, we see the importance of growth or change at a steady, measured pace. Remember Nehemiah again. He only asked the people to build six inches of wall per day.

BENEFITS OF STARTING SMALL

Starting small allows us to do pilot testing and float "trial balloons" before making a larger commitment. Also, we tend to get less pushback from people comfortable with the status quo. We observe businesses doing this all the time. HCA piloted new computer software before large-scale rollouts. Restaurants pilot new menus in key markets before making nationwide changes.

George Barna wrote a book titled *The Frog in the Kettle*.[23] He explained how you can put a frog in a kettle of water and turn the heat on. Because the water warms up slowly, the frog will not jump out of the kettle and will boil to death.

Let's take a simple example. If I had a 300-page book and asked people to read it, many would feel overwhelmed. They would begin to explain how busy they were and how it would be nearly impossible for them to read the book with everything else going on. If I gave them the same book and asked if they could take ten minutes and read ten pages that day or evening, most people would say yes. If I did that for thirty days, they would have read the 300-page book. I have actually used this approach to get feedback on this book as I have written it. I have asked people to read a section at a time and give feedback rather than read the whole book at one time.

Often, the reason for procrastination is that people feel overwhelmed at the size of the project. That's why it is so important to take big projects and break them into small pieces. Remember my example earlier of leading changes at the audit team? When the team worked together to take big initiatives and break them into small projects, there was no pushback to moving forward.

The TV industry has used a gradual approach to impact our culture and society significantly, though I don't think in a positive way. When I had children and started watching reruns of programs from when I was a kid and then watched network TV, I was struck at the change in the language, the violence, the sexual innuendos, and the overall values over thirty years. If the programming we watched today had been aired thirty years ago in this nation, there would have been a rebellion, and families would have turned off their TVs. But because the change in programming was done gradually, it never reached the tipping point in a given year where people would have rebelled and quit watching.

This principle works in computer conversions. After computer software is changed, it is implemented in a pilot. It stays in the pilot until all the bugs are worked out. It saves considerable time and cost to pilot new software rather than immediately implementing it on a broad scale. Imagine the time and costs required to fix computer bugs at multiple locations. HCA went through a major computer conversion one time, involving the over three hundred hospitals we operated. We went through the process of pilot testing the new system and made numerous modifications. Imagine the time, cost, and disruption to the operations and the resistance to change if we had implemented the new software in three hundred facilities without first doing a pilot in one. Pilot projects are designed so that they are not overwhelming.

Starting small, "pilot testing," increases efficiency over the long run because problems are avoided. When national restaurant chains want to change their menus, what do they do? They take a restaurant or a market and pilot the change. They see the reaction to the change. They make any needed modifications and re-test. Then they begin to roll the new items out to all their restaurants. If the change is not successful, they haven't failed in three thousand restaurants. They've failed in one restaurant or in one market. Any changes needed are made in the pilot and not in three thousand restaurants.

Let's assume a certain restaurant were changing three menu items. They do it in one restaurant and change one menu. Two of the items are very successful, and the third isn't. So they change the menu universally to include only the two successful items. It costs much less to experiment in one restaurant versus three thousand restaurants.

Leading change in Physician Services

In leading Physician Services, we used the principles of the mustard seed and yeast to expand our initiatives significantly over several years. One example was the recruiting function for physicians. We took one market where there was a desire to consolidate the recruiting efforts. Our team did that with good success. We built on that success and went to other markets in that division. The division was having better success than other divisions in that group. We then went to another division within the group and had good results there as well. After some time, we had implemented the change in all divisions in that group.

Then we went to another group and showed them the results. There was one division within that group that wanted to pilot the program. We implemented it with good results. The other divisions followed within the group until we were running the program in all divisions in that group. Over three to four years, we implemented the program across the entire company. If we had tried to implement that program as one big initiative, it would have never gotten national-level support and would have never happened.

We implemented a hospitalist initiative by working with one group president. He put an individual on his payroll, and we performed the management oversight. The results were very good at the hospitals in his group. Then we were able to put the manager on our payroll and promote the initiative on a broader basis. Success always breeds more success. We would go to hospitals that wanted to implement the initiative. We communicated the successful results, and soon other hospitals wanted the program. We began managing all the contracted vendors for hospitalists. If this had been presented as a national initiative from the beginning, it would have never gotten the support.

We did a similar thing, but in a different way, with a hospital-based anesthesia initiative. I believed we were paying too much in anesthesia subsidies because we did not have enough expertise at the local level in many situations. We found an individual who was very qualified but couldn't get the approval to put that individual on the payroll. I talked to one division president who was always good to work with and had a big opportunity in this area. I asked him if he would do a pilot where we contracted with this person to do the anesthesia contracting and negotiation as a consultant. I said Physician Services would pay half if his division would pay half. We had enough room in the budget for the consulting fee but couldn't get approval for an added person on the payroll.

We ran the pilot for six months and saved so much money in anesthesia subsidies that we were able to get approval to hire the person full-time. We did a lot of work and that division showed substantial results. Then we went to other divisions within that group with great results. Over three years, we developed an extensive team and did work throughout the company with many millions of dollars in savings. Without a creative, low-risk approach, this initiative would not have gotten started.

Over twelve years, we added a number of service lines and major initiatives within the Physician Services function. They all had national influence, but every one was started as a pilot and implemented throughout the company gradually. There's not a single one that we could have sold as a national initiative from the beginning.

Another thing that was very important was giving other people the credit at every opportunity. We were most effective when pointing to an operational success that we were part of rather than trying to take the credit for an initiative. After a successful pilot, we would point to Operations and give them all the credit.

> *"Do not claim honor in the presence of the King, and do not stand in the place of great men."*
> *Proverbs 25:6*

Our role in the process was always ultimately revealed, and we were given the opportunity to help the next set of operators. Small pilots became very large initiatives over time using this approach.

Warning – "Idea of the Week" Leaders

Some leaders see themselves as change agents when, in fact, they are simply "idea of the week" leaders. Most organizations of any size have one somewhere. They go by different names, but this is a common one. Change for the sake of change without a clear plan and use of "pilots" to monitor success is not the way to implement change.

Some leaders say the process or people are not working out, and they begin making changes without the counsel of others and without a plan. This often results in no improvement or in the situation getting even worse. Too much change, change not well planned, or change that the team has not been involved in is usually going to yield poor results.

Entrepreneurial leaders in for-profit and non-profit organizations can do this a lot. They are often creative by nature, get bored easily, and make changes for the sake of change. There are certain personality profiles that are highly creative and have problems with the status quo. Sometimes they will make unnecessary changes. There is a difference between leaders who promote continual change programs toward a "vision" and creative leaders who are often referred to as "idea of the week" or "idea of the month" leaders.

PEOPLE

Chapter 21

DOCUMENT AND TRAIN

> Thought:
> Have you considered how much time you could save if what you knew was well documented and people were trained?

"Now these things happened as examples for us, so that we would not crave evil things as they also craved."

1 Corinthians 10:6

Dr. Frist, Sr. used to say that mankind started making its most significant progress after we learned to write. In fact, there was a significant change among mankind after the invention of the printing press. Being able to document what we have learned so that each generation doesn't have to "reinvent the wheel" has been significant to our progress. One reason God had men write the Bible was so that we could learn from the lives and mistakes of others and wouldn't have to learn everything based on our own experience. This is what I Corinthians 10:6 (above) is talking about.

We see the same thing in organizations. When I led the internal audit department, one of the things we dealt with was turnover. Even though it improved, it was still high compared to other corporate functions. That was the nature of the internal audit department because it was used as a training ground and promotional opportunity for many professionals. As we tried to add value to the company through our work, I began to hire specialists in certain areas. They would do great work and take our capabilities to new levels.

They would normally stay about two years before someone else in the company hired them because of their specialized knowledge. Then it felt like we would start all over again with someone new.

So I made the commitment that we would have heavy documentation of everything our specialists knew. We created detailed audit programs. We added supplements to the audit programs that explained in detail the thought process and best methods for completing each step. We designed preprinted work papers to facilitate the consistent gathering of information. Once we did this, we did not lose all the expertise of the person that moved somewhere else in the company. In fact, the replacement was able to get up to speed very quickly and usually improved on what we had already developed.

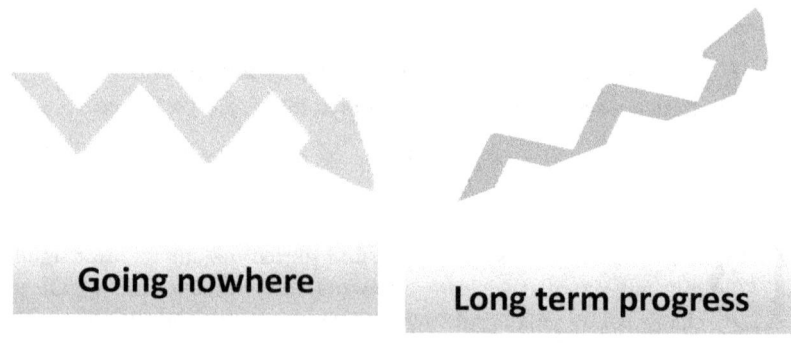

Going nowhere   **Long term progress**

Following this protocol helped us avoid the peaks and valleys in the quality of our work. Over time our expertise grew and we performed at higher levels. As our department grew we added staff and multiple trained individuals, which was also important for the retention of knowledge. Without good documentation and training, organizations cannot maintain a consistent standard of performance or grow their expertises.

This is one of the reasons small organizations stay small. Everything is known by a few people, and the organization can't grow beyond what they personally know and oversee. Documentation allows an organization to develop and learn from best practices, continue to improve, and efficiently train and engage others in the process so that the organization grows. This is one thing that makes franchise models so successful.

When documentation and training are done properly, the new hires don't start from scratch. They begin with the documented knowledge of the previous job holders and often are able to add their unique perspectives and experience to improve the results. It's much quicker and more efficient to bring people up to speed with good documents.

EXAMPLE

A manager in one doctor's office I'm familiar with told me she was frequently distracted from her work by employees bringing problems to her. I asked her what the top three issues were. She told me and I said that all three could be solved by some training. She was already working a lot of hours, but she took time each week to train her staff. After two weeks and only two hours of training, she was saving two hours per week. Good training yields a very high return in the time it ultimately saves.

PEOPLE

Chapter 22

CREATE ENABLING CONTROL SYSTEMS

> **Thought:**
> How much more could you relax if you had an easy way of knowing that things in your organization were under control? If you had a system to keep things on track, how much time and energy would you save?

"So then each one of us will give an account of himself to God."

Romans 14:12

One of the great challenges many entrepreneurs face is empowering others and letting go appropriately. They do not know how to empower yet keep control. The behavior I see ranges from micromanaging with a "thumb in every pie" to giving instructions and never following up on the end result.

If we are going to be godly leaders, we should look at how God handles the issue of control. In this area, I see two extremes in how people think about God. There are those who believe that God is an over-controlling micromanager who does everything He can to make sure we do not enjoy life, punishes us every time we get off track, and wants to keep us from doing what we really want to do. Then there are those who believe God is uninterested and uninvolved and that everything in life happens according to chance. One theme in the Forrest Gump movie was, "Life is like a box of chocolates. You never know what you're going to get."

Let's look at this through Scripture to see how God empowers but also controls appropriately. The fact that God empowers is clear in the creation account.

After everything was created, Scripture says God gave man dominion over the garden and every living creature (Genesis 1:28). That seems like a God who empowers. He lets go. He gives people freedom with His creation.

So what about control? In the beginning, God only had one rule. That was to not eat from the tree of the knowledge of good and evil (Genesis 2:17). In fact, God said Adam and Eve could eat of any tree and any plant in the garden, but not of that one single tree. That doesn't seem like micromanagement to me. There was only one rule. And what was the purpose of the rule? Was the purpose to restrict their freedom? Was the purpose to restrict their enjoyment of paradise? No! The purpose was to protect them from what God knew would harm them. But they ate from the fruit of that tree. That act changed their way of life and excluded them from the beautiful garden.

Later, God gave people more rules, including the Ten Commandments. There are certain things we must do and things we are not to do. What was the purpose of the Ten Commandments? Following them works for our good. All ten commandments protect and preserve our relationship with God and enhance our relationship with others. God gave people these commands to protect them. The commands were to create more enjoyment and fulfillment in life, not less.

As time went on, God's people rebelled more, and God continued to give them direction through rules—always intended to guide and protect them. The rules were never controls for the sake of God's exerting His power, showing His strength or limiting the people's freedom and enjoyment of life. They were always to guide and protect—to keep people from hurting themselves or one another and to maximize their enjoyment of life. Jesus said, "I came that you might have life and have it more abundantly." Some translations say "have it to the full" (John 10:10).

When people were not lined up with God's mission but followed their own plans, He had to implement more rules to protect them against themselves. In our organizations, the less people are aligned with the mission, vision, and values, the more rules we have to make. It would be far better to have greater alignment so we could have fewer rules.

THE LESSON OF THE RIVER

I think we learn a lot about God through nature. A river reminds me of how God works. I sometimes ask people what a river has that other bodies of water do not. They quickly come to the conclusion that river has a current that gives it movement. Then they point out that the river has banks to guide it.

A river is made up of millions of drops of water that fall during a rain, run into streams, then run into creeks, and finally join the mighty river. The water is in motion. The banks of the river do not micromanage each drop of water but rather gently guide the river.

Now think of how a good organization functions. People, tasks, and activities are not micromanaged. Rather, they are guided gently by the boundaries in place in the organization toward its vision. What in an organization creates the current or movement? The organization's vision and the goals for each individual create the movement.

What creates the boundaries equivalent to the banks of river? There are several things, including: policies and procedures, operating manuals, standards for performance, training, and accountability systems.

Why should these be created? To enable individuals to accomplish the mission and vision of the organization. When done properly, leadership will know the status of all the things that impact the vitality of the organization. Some people and certain personality types like control just for the sake of exercising control. After many years of being an auditor, I have a firm belief that control systems should never be about control just for the sake of control. Nor should they limit an individual's freedom unless doing so protects people and is in the best interests of the organization.

SWAMP ANALOGY

If you took away the banks of a river, what would you have over time? It would become a swamp, wouldn't it? What is a swamp like? First of all, it stinks because the water has become stagnant. Next, it's very easy to get lost in a swamp because there is no flow of water or banks to give direction. Third, swamps are dangerous for human beings to try to live in. There are a lot of surprises in swamps, and almost none of them are positive.

Now let's think about what an organizational swamp would look like. I've been in a number of them in my organizational career. First, the culture stinks because everything is stagnant. Next, there is no flow or direction because the vision of the organization is not clear. And, finally, people are just trying to survive. They're lost and don't know how to get out, but don't feel safe staying in.

So how do you turn organizational swamps into rivers that have life, direction, and flow? Here is what I did in these situations. As a foundation, we created as a team clarity about why the organization existed—mission. Then, we discovered God's vision for what the organization should become. Next, we created strategies and tactics to accomplish the vision. Finally, those strategies and tactics were broken into goals for individuals, with an accountability system for achieving them. Doing this created energy and current for the organization. Then appropriate policies and procedures, operating manuals, training systems, and enabling control systems were put in place to guide people and activities.

ORGANIZATIONAL FLOODING

We just saw what happens if the river banks get too wide—an organizational swamp is created. Now let's look at what happens if the banks get too narrow. If you had a big river that was a mile wide and suddenly narrowed the banks down to half a mile, what would happen? That's right, flooding! Where there is too much water and the banks are too narrow, water moves outside the banks and creates damage in surrounding areas.

How does flooding in organizations occur? Usually large amounts of change are created that cannot be accommodated by the existing boundaries of the organization. When the boundaries are too narrow for the changes occurring, people try to achieve their goals by working around the existing boundaries, seeing them as barriers. Now instead of having control, the organization has lost control. I've seen this happen many times, and it's dangerous to the organization.

This issue of setting the boundaries and vision for the organization is very important. Remember, Scripture says where there is no vision, the people perish (Proverbs 29:18). In organizational life, if there is not a clear vision and the boundaries are too broad, the result is an organizational swamp. By contrast, if there's a clear vision and a lot of movement and change but the boundaries are not set appropriately, you have organizational flooding. In this situation people work around existing boundaries and all control is lost.

EMPOWERING WHILE HAVING CONTROL

This brings up the question of how you empower and set boundaries. Do you empower people and never follow up to hold them accountable? In Lee Iacocca's book, he describes his turnaround efforts at Chrysler.[24] One thing he did was quarterly reviews or accountability sessions with each of his vice presidents. This is a practice I adapted and with good results. Using this method properly, it's not possible to go more than ninety days with your direct reports being off-track toward their annual goals without your knowing it. Of course, I had more frequent contact and follow-up, but these quarterly reviews were comprehensive in nature. At the end of the year, they had already had three reviews with me regarding their progress. Therefore, the annual review was easy to accomplish, and there were no surprises.

Finally, let's talk about how you set the boundaries. Whom do you engage in setting the boundaries and what is your attitude and motive? This brings us back to Chapter 11 of this book where we looked at personality profiles. The "D" profile likes to feel in control but doesn't like getting into details and will tend to delegate the establishment of policies and procedures, operating manuals, and controls. The "I" personality doesn't like getting into the details and tends to feel controls are abusive. The "S" personality is good at developing operating manuals and knowing how things are done and will appropriately engage in the development of manuals, policies and procedures, and controls. The "C" personality will tend to be more detail-oriented and risk-averse, and will design very tight controls. In many larger organizations, the "C" personality will volunteer to create the boundaries. The problem is when you don't have all four personality profiles involved, you will tend to get boundaries too narrow and the flow of the organization will actually be restricted. Then people simply comply and are not creative and proactive, or they rebel, work around the system, and you have less control.

It is a given that you can over-control and hinder progress. We have already discussed that. However, good and well-balanced control systems help detect problems early before they get too big, and they help keep us on track toward meaningful progress. What does a control system look like? From my experience, the simpler, the better. HCA had operating indicator reports that showed the standard, actual, and variance. Varying degrees of follow-up were initiated based on the degree of variance and its impact.

Why Expectations Are Not Met

Some things are easy to express in a measurable standard, and some are a bit harder. The most common reasons expectations are not met are these:

- The expectation is not clear, or the employee did not understand the expectation or how it would be measured.
- There are too many expectations, and some do not get proper emphasis.
- The expectation gap is not followed up on in a timely manner by the leader.

Follow-up in a reasonable timeframe is key in making sure expectations are clear. Any gap in understanding can be resolved so that you do not go for an extended period of time with an important expectation being unmet. One of the biggest reasons leaders do not get the expected results is that they do not follow up to ensure an expectation is met or some plan of action is created.

Chapter 23

CREATE PROGRESS THROUGH MEASUREMENT

> **Thought:**
> How much easier would your work be and how much more in control would you feel if you had a few measurable indicators telling you what you need to know?

"Immediately the one who had received the five talents went and traded with them, and gained five more talents."

Matthew 25:16

We like to keep score. We can't go to a kids T-ball game where the scores are not officially kept and not try to keep up with it in our heads. Keeping score gives us a sense of accomplishment. Would you keep playing golf if you couldn't keep score? Would you keep watching sports if scores weren't kept? Of course not. We have this innate need to create and be productive. Keeping score lets us know how we're doing. Measuring and reporting the right things can have substantial impact on the progress of an organization. Measuring the wrong things can hurt an organization.

Jack Welch once said at an HCA leadership conference, "If you can't measure it, you can't manage it." That's certainly true in organizations. It impacts people if measurements are communicated and followed up. So what do you measure? The simple answer is you measure the high priorities—those things that move the needle.

Scripture says that God numbers the hairs on my head (Luke 12:7). We are enough like our Creator that built within us is the desire to keep score. I know some people in ministry who give the impression that keeping score is not good. Yet these people are like all the other parents at the kids' T-ball games. T-ball is for the very young kids where the coaches don't keep score. Yet every parent there, including the ministers, know if their team won. Measuring results is just built into us. Imagine going to a football game or basketball game and not keeping score. How much fun would any sports activities be if scores were not kept? Have you noticed how frequently the score of the game is displayed on the TV screen?

Some would say spiritually that score keeping is wrong, and I will be the first to acknowledge that keeping score can be done wrong and do damage. Yet in the parable of the talents, score was kept and the stewards were rewarded for multiplying their investments. Peter asked Jesus what he and others would get for forsaking all and following Him. Jesus did not rebuke him. Instead, He said Peter would receive a hundred times what he had given up. If we are keeping score only to show that we beat someone else, perhaps that is unhealthy competition. But in Scripture, accomplishment is commanded, commended, and rewarded.

So how do we keep score in organizations? An organization has measures it tracks daily, weekly, monthly, and annually. It knows exactly where it stands against expectations for those timeframes. How about the employees? Do they know how they're doing within defined time intervals? If you don't keep score and provide feedback, they are likely to experience some anxiety or insecurity that is not necessary if they are doing well.

You may say, "We can't measure everything we want the employee to accomplish." This is particularly true in certain complex leadership roles. You can, however, give feedback on as much objective data as possible, as well as your perspective on performance versus expectations. Lee Iacocca did this quarterly with his vice president team when he turned Chrysler around.

I adopted Iacocca's approach at the vice president level in my organizations and believed it added to the focus, accomplishment, and lack of surprises and disappointments in the annual review process. The frequency of reviews really depends on the role, the concrete data available, and the personality of the individual—that is, the one being reviewed. Some people like broad measures over longer periods of time. Others tend to need more frequent feedback and affirmation.

WHAT SHOULD WE TRY TO MEASURE?

What we should measure is tied directly to the mission, values, vision, and priorities of the organization. Special focus should be placed on the priorities that have been agreed upon for the next year. When establishing measures, keep in mind what really "moves the needle." You're far better off having a few key measures to narrow the focus of what contributes most toward your vision. Think about how a river works. The narrower the banks are, the faster the water flows.

One mistake leaders sometimes make is not having balanced measures. If we measure quantity but not quality, we tend to produce poor quality goods or services. If we only measure quality but not quantity, we tend to be less productive. If our focus is only on cost and trying to reduce it, we may negatively impact quality.

I've seen numerous examples of new initiatives in organizations where measures are not kept in balance. One company did a massive computer conversion where the information technology department was incentivized based on the number of conversions, but not the quality or the downstream costs to the revenue cycle of a poor conversion.

In Physician Services, as we rolled out new service lines, one of the things we had to keep in balance was how quickly we rolled something out while maintaining the quality of the program. There were times when hospital or division operators wanted something done very quickly. Responding to those requests and doing things more quickly than we knew was prudent always caused problems that we had to fix. In the end, it took longer than doing it right in the first place.

Often, our leadership in Physician Services found themselves working hard to put the brakes on programs so we could implement them at a speed that would not create additional problems.

MICRO-MANAGERS VS. CONTROL SYSTEMS

Leaders of small organizations tend to limit themselves to what they can personally oversee. One reason they want to be so personally engaged is to have a sense of control. Yet a clearly established measurable standard and a reporting system to identify progress and exceptions gives leaders control over more than just what they can see. That doesn't mean that "management by walking around" isn't a good idea. It is. (Leaders walking around and observing are informal tools of measurement. Plus, there are benefits to the leaders being engaged beyond the measurement and control system aspect of management.)

THE CHAIN IS NO STRONGER THAN ITS WEAKEST LINK

I saw this principle applied at HCA one time in the area of accounts receivable. As a company, the days of accounts receivable were just too high. The average for the company may have been in the seventy to eighty range. Leadership thought fifty-five was a reasonable standard. So what did they do? Simply announce that fifty-five was the standard? What would that change? They did do some promotion and fanfare. They printed stickers and created banners that said, "Stay alive at 55." But what began to change things was the publishing of results and comparison of the operating units. Now that there was a contest, about 10% of the business office managers in the company wanted to have the lowest days of accounts receivable. So, they started working on ways to improve the results. And they did. After eighteen months, the top business office managers had their days of accounts receivable average less than forty.

What about the others? Well, some of those business office managers began to learn from those who had better results. Their days in accounts receivable went down as well. In some divisions, training programs were implemented and several of the business office managers improved their results. In some cases, business office managers were not able to learn enough from others or the training programs to improve the results; some looked for easier jobs, and others were asked to leave.

Here was the dynamic I observed. When the worst days in receivable in a division were ninety, the office manager at eighty or eighty-five was comfortable. When the worst came down to their level, they got really busy looking for ways to improve. The end result after eighteen months was that the worst hospital was at fifty-five days, and the company average was about forty-seven.

So let's make application to organizational life. Who sets the performance standard? Most operating managers would quickly say management does. I ask, "How?" They say, "We set the performance goals and standards." I ask, "Are they always met?" Rarely does anyone ever say yes. So I ask again, "Then who is setting the standard?" The real answer is the "weakest link in the chain." It is the people known to have the lowest level of performance and who continue to keep their jobs in the organization. The reason is that as long as everyone else can look at those people and know they're doing better, they feel safe. And that is fine as long as those people's levels of performance are acceptable.

The bottom line is this: to get improvement, do these things:

- Measure and publish results;
- Create a contest where the top performers can compete;
- Create opportunities for the lowest performers to learn from others;
- Offer training to help people meet the performance standards; and
- Make a change in personnel if people are not qualified for the job.

All of these tactics have their place in an organization. They produce tangible results when used correctly.

PEOPLE

Chapter 24

SUMMARY

So which will it be for you? Will people be your greatest asset or biggest headache? The answer to that really depends on you. It depends on decisions you make about people and how you view them. It depends on whether you will try to give them what they want and need and then get what the organization needs.

- It depends on what you expect from people and how you express those expectations.
- Are you going to take the time to really know your people and understand their unique personalities as you choose the right people for the team?
- Are you going to evaluate the team regularly to see if the key people still fit where the organization is going?
- Do you know how to help underperformers and influence motivation positively?

PEOPLE

- Can you delegate effectively and create a culture that empowers?
- Will you lead change constructively and provide documentation and training? Will you create enabling control systems or oppressive ones?
- Do you know what to measure and how to share it to increase the team's enjoyment and inspire them to higher levels of performance?

If you can do these things well, you'll be surprised at how much joy you can derive through leading, how much progress you can make, and how much your team will appreciate you. Many times leaders are frustrated because of their own shortcomings in how they get what they need from people. Don't let that be you.

Image Credits

Diana Rush–Organizational charts and DISC graphics
Clip art and photos are taken from Microsoft Word stock images, unless otherwise noted below or in the endnotes:

Page 45–Checkerboard–Kritchamut Onmang/DepositPhotos.com/©2015
Page 79–Puzzle man–Dan Barbalata/DepositPhotos.com/©2015
Page 92–Square peg–Santalucia Art, Inc./DepositPhotos.com/©2015

Cover Design—Darrel Girardier/©2015

ENDNOTES Part 1

Note #	Reference	Text Page
1	Charles R. Swindoll, *Living the Psalms* (Brentwood, TN: Worthy Publishing, 2012), page 233.	Page 5
2	Viktor E. Frankl, 1905-1997; Austrian neurologist, psychiatrist, and Holocaust survivor; quote attributed. Available from http://www.goodreads.com/author/quotes/2782.Viktor_E_Frankl	Page 6
3	Viktor E. Frankl, *Man's Search for Meaning* (Boston: Beacon Press, 1959).	Page 7
4	Rick Warren, *The Purpose Driven Life*, (Grand Rapids, Michigan: Zondervan, 2002).	Page 7
5	I learned much and clarified much of my understanding about franchises through my discussions with SteveLynn, former CEO of Sonic and Backyard Burgers.	Page 11
6	Robert Kiyosaki, *The Key to Hiring Right*, April 30, 2006. Available from Entrepreneur.com. http://www.entrepreneur.com/article/160158#	Page 29
7	Erica Olsen, *How to Write a Strategic Plan*, May 11, 2010, page 1. Available from http://mystrategicplan.com/resources/how-to-write-a-strategic-plan	Page 30
8	David Grusenmeyer, *Mission, Vision, Values & Goals*, page 2. Available from https://www.msu.edu/~steind/estate%20Goals%20Mission%20Values%20Overview_Pro-Dairy%2017pg.pdf	Page 30
9	David Grusenmeyer, *Mission, Vision, Values & Goals*, page 2. Available from https://www.msu.edu/~steind/estate%20Goals%20Mission%20Values%20Overview_Pro-Dairy%2017pg.pdf	Page 30
10	Erica Olsen, *How to Write a Strategic Plan*, May 11, 2010, page 1. Available from http://mystrategicplan.com/resources/how-to-write-a-strategic-plan	Page 30
11	*Mapping a Clear Organization Direction*, Triaxia Partners, Inc., page 4. Available from http://triaxiapartners.com/corp/strategy/articles/Mapping-Clear-Org-Figure	Page 30

Credits and Endnotes

12	David Grusenmeyer, *Mission, Vision, Values & Goals*, page 2. Available from https://www.msu.edu/~steind/estate%20Goals%20Mission%20Values%20Overview_ProDairy%2017pg.pdf	Page 31
13	*Mapping a Clear Organization Direction*, Triaxia Partners, Inc., page 1. Available from http://triaxiapartners.com/corp/strategy/articles/Mapping-Clear-Org-Figure	Page 31
14	David Grusenmeyer, *Mission, Vision, Values & Goals*, pages 4 and 5. Available from https://www.msu.edu/~steind/estate%20Goals%20Mission%20Values%20Overview_ProDairy%2017pg.pdf	Page 31
15	*Mapping a Clear Organization Direction*, Triaxia Partners, Inc., page 3. Available from http://triaxiapartners.com/corp/strategy/articles/Mapping-Clear-Org-Figure	Page 31
16	Andy Stanley, *Visioneering* (New York: Doubleday Religious Publishing Group, 2005), page 41.	Page 31
17	Peter Drucker, *The Practice of Management*. (New York: Harper Collins, Inc., 1954, 1982).	Page 32
18	Greg Coker, *Building Cathedrals – The Power of Purpose* (Chicago Spectrum Press, 20 (My rendition of this story doesn't exactly match the book "Building Cathedrals" by Greg Coker but is more like I remember it from the sermon I first heard it in. . I later discovered that this story is three hundred years old and has been told many times.)	Page 34
19	Zig Ziglar and Tom Ziglar, *Born To Win—Find Your Success Code* (Dallas: SUCCESS Media, 2012), page 3.	Page 44

# ENDNOTES Part 2

Note #	Reference	Text Page
1	Dan Miller, *No More Dreaded Mondays* (New York: Random House, 2009).	Page 50
2	Stephen Covey, *The 7 Habits of Highly Effective People*, (New York: Simon & Schuster, 1989).	Page 50
3	Belle Learning System	Page 61
4	From the movie *Cool Hand Luke*, spoken by the prison warden.	Page 68
5	About.com, *Inspirational Quotes for Business: Team Building*, by Susan M. Heathfield, page 1. Available from http://humanresources.about.com/od/inspirationalquotations/a/quotes_team.htm	Page 78
6	Robert Kiyosaki, *The Key to Hiring Right*, April 30, 2006. Available from Entrepreneur.com. http://www.entrepreneur.com/article/160158#	Page 78
7	Jim Collins, *Good to Great* (New York: Harper Collins, 2001).	Page 7
8	Dick Wells, *16 Stones* (Franklin, TN: New Vantage Publishing Partners, 2012).	Page 81
9	Dan Miller, *No More Dreaded Mondays* (New York: Random House, 2009).	Page 84
10	Monster.com, Management Skills: How to Deal with Poor Employee Performance? Available from http://hiring.monster.com/hr/hr-best-practices/workforce-management/employee-performance-management/emploee-performance-issues.aspx	Page 92
11	Monster.com, Management Skills: How to Deal with Poor Employee Performance? Available from http://hiring.monster.com/hr/hr-best-practices/workforce-management/employee-performance-management/emploee-performance-issues.aspx	Page 94
12	Jim Patton, *Life in the Turn Lane*, (Franklin, TN: New Vantage Books, 2010).	Page 95
13	Harvey Mackay, *Swim With the Sharks Without Being Eaten Alive*, (New York, NY: Harper Collins Publishers Inc., 1988, 2005).	Page 99

Credits and Endnotes

14	TerminatingEmployees.org, *Terminating Employees with a Professional Attitude,* page 1. NYSSCPA.org, "Ten Practical Suggestions for Terminating an Employee," by Chauncey M. DePree, Jr. and Rebecca K. Jude, pages 2 and 3. Available from http://www.nysscpa.org/cpajournal/2007/807/essentials/p62.htm	Page 108
15	TerminatingEmployees.org, *Terminating Employees with a Professional Attitude,* page 1. NYSSCPA.org, "Ten Practical Suggestions for Terminating an Employee," by Chauncey M. DePree, Jr. and Rebecca K. Jude, pages 2 and 3. Available from http://www.nysscpa.org/cpajournal/2007/807/essentials/p62.htm	Page 108
16	Monster.com, *Management Skills: How to Deal with Poor Employee Performance?* Available from http://hiring.monster.com/hr/hr-best-practices/workforce-management/employee-performance-management/employee-performance-issues.aspx	Page 108
17	Dan Miller, *No More Dreaded Mondays* (New York: Random House, 2009).	Page 115
18	"Teacher Expectations and Labeling," Article by Christine Rubie-Davies. Springer International Handbooks of Education, 2009, Volume 21, page 695-707. Available from http://link.springer.com/chapter/10.1007%2F978-0-387-73317-3_43#page-1	Page 122
19	"Teachers' Expectations Can Influence How Students Perform," article by Alix Spiegel, September 17, 2012. Available from http://www.npr.org/blogs/health/2012/09/18/161159263/teachers-expectations-can-influence-how-students-perform	Page 122
20	Simplypsychology.org, *Skinner – Operant Conditioning,* by Saul McLeod, page 1. Available from http://www.simplypsychology.org/operant-conditioning.html	Page 122
21	Dick Wells, *16 Stones* (Franklin, TN: New Vantage Publishing Partners, 2012).	Page 143
22	Dick Wells, *16 Stones* (Franklin, TN: New Vantage Publishing Partners, 2012).	Page 146
23	George Barna, *The Frog in the Kettle* (Ada, MI: Baker Publishing Group, Inc., 1990)	Page 148
24	Lee Iacocca, *Iacocca: An Autobiography,* (New York: Bantam/Random House, 1984, 2007), pages 50-52.	Page 161

Notes

Enjoy additional books by Leon Drennan and Vision Leadership Foundation
Please visit www.vision-leadership.com

You can be a great leader, or a royal pain . . .

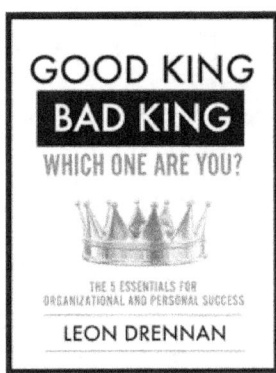

Good King/Bad King captures the essence of excellent leadership and reveals what it takes to live abundantly through five principles of visionary, profitable, and significant leadership. Whether you serve in a for-profit business, a church, nonprofit, or government, the blessing you bring to the people in your care and the organization you lead will make them grateful for your position in their lives. Let Leon Drennan's counsel and guidance show where you are on the path to leading with grace and skill, and inspire your noble pursuit of fine leadership.

Reap while you grow!

LIFE CAN OVERFLOW with the warmth and exuberance of spring or the lavish blessing of a late summer harvest. Other times, the bitter cold of loneliness, loss, or failure leaves you lifeless and desolate. Whatever the season, God can bring a harvest of blessing if you discover what He has for you in each. In *Seasons of the Soul*, Leon Drennan shows how to recognize which season you're experiencing and how to respond to God. If you cooperate with the Master Planner, you can even make the good seasons last longer and the bad seasons end sooner. God will never be one bit harder on you or provide one less miracle than you need. So dig in to this book, and reap a spiritual bounty—whatever your season.

www.ingramcontent.com/pod-product-compliance
Lightning Source LLC
Chambersburg PA
CBHW070613300426
44113CB00010B/1515